SATTERFIELD ON THE LOOSE

Being a compendium of essays and observations from the author's *Journal Star* columns and comprised of the truth, mainly.

LEON SATTERFIELD

You don't know about me, without you have read a book by the name of The Adventures of Tom Sawyer, *but that ain't no matter. That book was made by Mr. Mark Twain, and he told the truth, mainly. There was things which he stretched, but mainly he told the truth.*

—Opening paragraph of Mark Twain's
The Adventures of Huckleberry Finn

J&L Lee Co.
Lincoln, Nebraska

Much of this book has appeared in the *Lincoln Star* and the *Journal Star* in variously edited forms. Grateful acknowledgment is made for their permission to reprint.

ISBN 0-934904-39-1

987654321

J & L Lee Co.
P.O. Box 5575
Lincoln, NE 68505

www.binary.net/leebooks/

e-mail: leebooks@radiks.net
1-888-655-0999

A Cautionary Note to the Reader

The following pieces were written, beginning in the spring of 1990, as every-other-Monday columns in *The Lincoln Star*, and later in *The Lincoln Journal-Star*.

Some of them purport to be humorous, so whatever you do, do not try to read them all at once. An overdose of purported humor is no fun.

I once taught a semester-long course in American humor. We read and talked about nothing except the funniest of the funny stuff American humorists have produced from the 17th century on. The first couple of weeks we laughed so hard that bodily fluids came out our noses.

But it was all downhill from then until the end of the semester. By the last several weeks, we'd worked our way up to what I thought would be the crescendo of hilarity that would end the course: wonderfully funny 20th-century writers like James Thurber and Ring Lardner and H. L. Mencken. But the whole class was dozing by then.

In Russell Baker's introduction to his 1993 anthology of American humor, he writes "When you are creeping through the literary underbrush hoping to bag a piece of humor with your net, nothing seems funny. The thing works the other way around. Humor is funny when it sneaks up on you and takes you by surprise. When you stalk it . . . the effect is narcotic."

So to avoid putting you to sleep, I have mixed in some leavening pieces that purport to be deeply profound. My wife says she can't always tell the purported profundity from the purported humor, and that it might be a good idea to accompany each piece with an appropriate pictograph, say a smily face or a furrowed-browed face.

That strikes me as lacking literary dignity, so I haven't done it.

Creeping Charlie

JUNE 16, 1997

This is the summer I'm surrendering unconditionally to the Creeping Charlie. I've given it bits and pieces before, but now it's the whole yard.

You know what Creeping Charlie is. It's that spreading, cloverish, ground-covery stuff that really likes growing in Lincoln—sun or shade, acid or alkali—in much the way kudzu really likes growing in Mississippi, the main difference being that Creeping Charlie won't grow up your nostrils while you sleep in the hammock. It doesn't attack. It creeps.

And in May and June, it has those sensual little blue flowers to make sure everyone notices it isn't Kentucky bluegrass.

When I tell people I'm surrendering my yard to Creeping Charlie, they smile uneasily—as if I've just told them I'm going to stop clipping the hair that grows out of my ears and nose.

They see my surrender as a character defect, a sign that in my dotage I've given up respectability. Next, they probably imagine, I'll give up changing my socks and underwear.

Well, they're wrong.

I'm letting the Creeping Charlie have my yard as a matter of principle. It's another manifestation of my dirty rotten secular humanist rebellion against Puritanism.

You don't see the connection? Stay with me a minute on this.

When the Puritans came to Massachusetts in the 1620s, they brought with them their great admiration for the Doctrine of Original Sin. "In Adam's fall," they'd fondly tell their children, "we sinned all."

An important part of the doctrine was that while everything was lovely in the Garden of Eden before Adam and Eve ate the apple, it's all been pretty nasty ever since. Before the apple, it was eternal springtime, animals all got along with each other, there was no kudzu. After the apple, Adam had to go to work, Eve had to have babies, animals got all snarly, Russian thistles popped up like dandelions. Nature turned mean.

And that perceived adversity invigorated the Puritans, made them feel even more martyred. So when they came to the New World, their leader, William Bradford, was pleased to report being surrounded by "a howling wilderness"—Nature unleavened by Calvinism.

The Puritans turned to the obvious remedy: they set about changing the howling wilderness into a great big lawn of Kentucky bluegrass.

And that's how we got where we are today, much to the profit of the fertilizer-pesticide-herbicide complex that has played on our Puritan fear of the natural to convince us that a good lawn is a triumph of virtuous chemistry over wicked Nature.

Sex is also part of wicked Nature—hence, H. L. Mencken's definition of Puritanism as "the haunting fear that someone somewhere is having a good time"—and so we cut our Kentucky bluegrass before it can flower or go to seed. As Michael Pollan noted in a *New York Times* essay, "lawns are nature purged of sex."

And in my secular humanist rebellion, I say to hell with all that.

Not that I'm averse to Kentucky bluegrass. It probably grows in Kentucky the way Creeping Charlie grows in Lincoln—effortlessly, naturally, the way Nature intended it to grow.

But I've given up growing Kentucky bluegrass in my yard for the same reason I've given up growing porpoises in my rain barrel. From now on, I grow only what wants to be grown. I no longer shake my fist at Nature.

For those who say I'm just quitting like a quitter, that this is all just a rationalization for my own laziness, I have a more powerful rationale for letting the Creeping Charlie have my yard. It's The Biblical Argument.

Here it is:

Creeping Charlie is divinely endorsed in the very first chapter of Genesis. Yes! It's when God is admiring the still-unspoiled perfection of the creation and proclaiming it good. On His list of good things, along with the fish of the sea, the fowl of the air, and so forth, is a more inclusive category: "every creeping thing that creepeth upon the earth."

Nothing there about Kentucky bluegrass that needeth mowing once a week, that needeth water and fertilizer and herbicide and pesticide even unto the end of time. Just every creeping thing that creepeth.

So letting the Creeping Charlie have my yard is a sacramental act. I'm recreating a little Eden, a small Paradise where, a little while after morning has broken like the first morning, while red bird's still singing like the first bird, I loll about in sweet surrender to the sensual little blue flowers of a pre-Puritan God's benevolence.

That's my story and I'm sticking to it.

Aging Angst

MAY 4, 1992

"O, O, O," I moan, dropping the "h" to indicate great passion. Anguish in this case.

"What now?" my wife asks. "You look like a Republican who just got trickled down on."

"O sure," I say. "Make jokes about the suffering. Ridicule the sore at heart. Guffaw at the afflicted."

"It's the log-splitter, isn't it?" she says. "You're worried that you've lost your manhood because of the hydraulic log-splitter."

She's right, of course. I've always liked that line in *Walden* where Thoreau says that "every man looks at his woodpile with a kind of affection." I have a woodpile and I not only look at it with affection, I'm crazy about it. I fondle my woodpile. I hum little celebratory hymns to it. I sit on the back porch and look at it long and long.

It's partly because I'm a tightwad and I like to think the woodpile represents stacks of money I'll save in heating my house. It's partly because I've got a touch of pyromania and the woodpile promises fire.

But it's mainly because splitting the wood with my 12-pound maul gives me a tremendous jolt of virility. I raise the maul over my head, then bring it down like a thunderbolt on the log. Thwack-o! And I'm 25 years old again, full of machismo and self-admiration. It's like a goat-gland transplant.

But last month I hurt my back and rented a hydraulic log-splitter instead. No thwack-o. No self-admiration. No goat gland. Just another machine doing the work I used to do for myself.

"So yeah," I say to my wife. "I guess it's partly the hydraulic log-splitter. And my torque wrench."

"Your torque wrench, of course," she says, hitting herself in the forehead. "How ever could I have missed the tragic significance of your torque wrench?"

I gave it to our younger son. He wanted to borrow it because he's still young enough to do his own work on his VW Beetle. So I gave him my torque wrench for his birthday—the kind of gift, my wife says, you'd expect from a tightwad.

"Here," I said, handing it to him and looking melancholy. "The torque is passed from the old generation to the new. Happy birthday."

I hadn't used it since 1977 when I bought it to tighten down head bolts after my older son and I replaced the blown head gasket on my '64 Mercedes diesel. We got so gloriously filthy that it became a male-bonding exercise, and the Mercedes actually ran for a little while after that. It was the high-water mark of the grease-under-my-fingernails stage of masculinity.

But engines don't make sense to me any more, sitting crosswise the way they do and thus throwing off my automotive geography so much that I can barely find the oil dipstick when I raise the hood. I feel like Orville Wright staring at the instrument panel of a 747, an abacus man peering into the innards of a Macintosh: I feel old.

"Is there anything else?" she asks. "Is it just the hydraulic log-splitter and the torque wrench? Or are there other deeply profound sources of your male aging angst?"

"Well, there is one more thing," I say, ducking my head and looking at my shoelaces. "It's . . . it's the hair growing out of my ears. I didn't used to have hair growing out of my ears. Only old men have hair growing out of their ears."

"There, there," she says, patting my bald spot. "Don't hold back. You'll feel better."

"O, O, O," I say again just before I lapse into the English teacher's last refuge, quoting someone else. "Where are the snows of yesteryear? With rue my heart is laden. Make way for Oedipus."

"Don't overreact," she says. "You didn't kill your father and marry your mother. You only rented a hydraulic log-splitter and gave away your torque wrench. And you have hair growing out of your ears. Lots of hair."

"I have heard the mermaids singing each to each," I tell her. "I do not think that they will sing to me."

"OK," she sighs—we've played this game before. "'Tis not too late to seek a newer world. The best is yet to be. Though we cannot make our sun stand still, yet we will make him run. Is that enough?"

I stop whimpering. She knows just what to say.

"You're a pretty good husband," she says, "but you do go on. Now let's eat. I'll cut up your meat for you."

She always knows just what to say.

Truth Serum

SEPTEMBER 14, 1992

Although it would come to be known as the most treacherous piece of political sabotage of the century, the press didn't find out about the president's sodium pentothal patch until the '92 election was over.

But all the pundits agreed that while his sudden burst of candor during the last week of the campaign made him oddly attractive, it lost him the election. The only state he carried was Nebraska. It was football season.

The truth serum had been osmosing through the president's pores since Oct. 26 when the patch had been surreptitiously stuck to the base of his spine by a female intern at Bethesda Naval Hospital. (He would later refer to her as "that nice lady doctor.") Wearing only his slippers and open-backed hospital gown for his monthly checkup, the president was taking the day off from campaigning, confident of the polls showing he had come back from a 23-point deficit to draw even with Gov. Clinton by mid-October. A week later, he had a five-point lead and the momentum was clearly his.

"Big mo," the president liked to say, pointing to himself. *"C'est moi!"*

The third time he said it on television, the intern was heard to say "We'll just see about that."

"Way to go, Mr. President," she told him when he said it again in the examination room. Then she slapped him on the bare backside with the sodium pentothal patch hidden in her hand. "Give 'em hell, Harry."

The first sign there might be something amiss came the next afternoon when the president told a conference of historians that when he got right down to it, he wasn't absolutely certain that he should take all the credit for the collapse of international communism.

"After all," he said, "containment had been a policy of both

Republicans and Democrats for decades. The commies just happened to go broke on my watch."

We know now that James Baker wrote him a sharply-worded memo questioning the strategy of that admission. But the president seemed unable to help himself. For the next week he ignored his prepared text when it deviated from what he knew to be the truth.

On the morning of Oct. 28, he told a group of Republican women that Hillary Clinton hadn't really written that marriage was a form of slavery, and the next day he told a national television audience that Gov. Clinton wasn't really proposing to raise taxes for everybody, only for people making more than $200,000 a year.

"My mistake," he said. "I don't know anyone who makes less than $200,000, so I thought he was talking about everybody. I could bite my tongue."

Marlin Fitzwater shook his head and rolled his eyes when reporters asked about it later.

On Oct. 30, the president told the National Association of Manufacturers that his earlier charge that Gov. Clinton had raised Arkansas taxes 128 times in 11 years was a "bogus campaign ploy because of the goofy way we were counting. If we counted our own tax increases the same way, we'd have to say there were 133 of them in just four years."

William Safire noted that the president seemed to be speaking in complete sentences more often, George Will said his words were "no longer just audible confetti," and Donald Kaul said the president was "suddenly sensible, even likable." "When George Bush vowed to do whatever was necessary to get re-elected," Mike Royko wrote, "nobody guessed he'd sink to telling the truth."

On the Sunday before the election, the president told the AMA he really had no health care plan beyond doing whatever the insurance companies wanted, and the next day he told the VFW that deep down he felt that even his foreign policy "sucked canal water." Nobody had heard him use that phrase before.

"Everybody says the Gulf War was such a success," he said, "but look at what it did: restored a corrupt Kuwaiti emir to his corrupt throne, killed several hundred thousand Iraqi people we had no quarrel with, and left the guy we went after still in power. If that's success, we ought to try failure. You know?"

Gov. Clinton was so confused by the president's candor that he cancelled all his speaking engagements the last four days before the election, thus increasing his popularity by 12 points. He remained speechless even after the president's remarkable seven-word concession.

"The hell with it," the chief magistrate told the nation. "I'm going fishing."

The patch lost its potency a few days later and by the time President Clinton was inaugurated, Citizen Bush was talking to Barbara about making another run in '96.

"I'd make a crackerjack president," he told her. "Don't you think?"

"It'll be all right," she said, patting his hand. "And isn't it about time to make another appointment with that nice lady doctor?"

Really Serious Cold

APRIL 22, 1996

This is going to be hard to believe, so brace yourself: For the fifth consecutive year now, I have the worst cold in the history of humankind.

I imagine it baffles the experts.

"Every year someone has the worst cold," some expert from the World Health Organization (Really Serious Cold Division) must be saying, "but I'm baffled that it should be the same man for five consecutive years."

"What really baffles me," a second expert must be saying, "is that in each of the last five years the standard by which we measure the worst cold in the history of humankind has gone up."

"Those are both very baffling phenomena," a third expert must be saying, "but the most baffling thing of all is that the afflicted man should suffer so nobly, so heroically, so bravely."

I gave my cold to my wife, but only after I'd sacrificially sifted out all the really nasty parts. You can tell she's not suffering nearly as much as I am because she doesn't cry out.

"You should be of good cheer," she says cheerfully. "These colds too shall pass."

"Not my cold," I say, "My cold is without end; it shall be with me always."

"Well," she says, "colds don't get better when you're full of self-pity. My cold shall pass."

"That's because," I explain as gently as I can, "yours is not a Really Serious Cold. The Dispenser of Colds inflicts on each of us no more than we can bear, and men can bear more than women. Why else would my cold have forced my back to go out while your back remains free of pain?"

The first day of my cold, I sneezed so hard I had to wash my face. When I leaned over the sink, I threw my back out. Now every time I sneeze, my back hurts.

"Ah-choo," I say. Then I say "Ow."

My wife laughs.

"You laugh at my pain?" I ask.

"I laugh at your noises," she says. "They're very funny noises."

"There's nothing funny about my back going out when I'm having the worst cold in the history of humankind," I say. "And for the fifth time in five years."

"How would you know?" she asks, thrusting an AP clipping in my face. "How would you remember last year's cold, much less one from five years ago?"

The clipping is from the April 11 *Journal-Star*, and the headline reads "Men's brains shrink during aging process." The story says the shrinkage curbs "memory, concentration, and reasoning power."

"What," I ask, "have I to do with this clipping, or this clipping to do with me?"

"Try to concentrate," she says. "Try to reason. Try to remember. You're an aging man. Your brain is shrinking. Your memory is curbed. So how can you remember how bad your cold was five years ago?"

"Sure," I say. "Scoff at the sick and infirm. Don't I remember your promising to pat my hand and say 'there, there' in sickness and in health?"

"Yet another figment of your diminished imagination," she says. "A result, perhaps, of your brain drying up and rattling around inside your head every time you sneeze. My brain, on the other hand, stays put when I sneeze because it's still moist, plump, and female."

"Oh, that's very scientific," I say. I can be quite sarcastic when my back is out and I can't breathe through my nose. "Your mystical woman's intuition, I suppose, tells you that."

"Yes," she says, "my woman's intuition and the Magnetic Resonance Imaging machine that shows men lose 15 percent of their frontal lobes and 8.5 percent of their temporal lobes by the time they're middle aged. Women, the AP says, 'lose tissue in neither lobe.'"

"What are you going to believe?" I ask. "Quack evidence from a clearly biased MRI widget? Or your daily encounters with this steel trap I call my mind?"

She laughs again. Colds make her all giddy.

"Pish tosh," she says with a cheery cough. "I'd tell you not to be so grumpy, but the article says you can't help it. As your brain shrinks, not only the memory, reasoning, and concentration parts dry up; so does the part that counteracts grumpiness."

"I'm not grumpy," I say, trying to straighten my back as I ease out of my recliner. "Dammitalltohellanyway."

The effort makes me sneeze.

"Ah-choo," I say. "Ow."

My brain rattles. My back hurts. My wife laughs. I blow my nose and lose another percent of my frontal lobe. Experts at the World Health Organization (Really Serious Cold Division) grow still more baffled.

Baby Shower

MARCH 9, 1992

Eat this column after you read it. I don't want it to get back to the boys in my hometown. It's about going to a baby shower.

It wasn't my fault. My daughter made me go. She's going to have a baby and she said I had to come to the baby shower.

"I can't," I said. "I'm a boy. Boys don't go to baby showers. Boys mess with John Deeres."

"You don't have a John Deere," she said. "You haven't messed with a John Deere since you were 19 years old. You have to come to the baby shower."

I was about to tell her that a man's gotta refuse to do what a man's gotta refuse to do, but she played hardball. If I didn't come to the baby shower, she said, I couldn't chuck her baby under the chin and say "Hey. Hey, there."

So I went. I was glad that none of the boys from my hometown were there.

When I was growing up back in the forties and fifties, boys in my hometown were afraid the same things would happen if they went to baby showers that would happen if they rode girls' bicycles: first they'd get interested in silk underwear, then they'd put on lipstick, and finally they'd no longer be anatomically correct.

But my wife tells me that the Baby Game has, thank God, changed. Now, she says, boys do lots of things they didn't used to do.

She reminds me that when our first grandbaby, Lovely Little Leslie Jo the Wonder Child, was born four months ago, our son was right there in the birthing room. That's what they're called now instead of delivery rooms, and fathers are invited to come on in.

Not only was our son in the birthing room, he was participating in the process, coaching our daughter-in-law in her breathing and pushing, and taking pictures of everything—including Lovely Little Leslie Jo when she was about ten seconds old and still needing a bath pretty bad.

Fathers didn't do anything like that when our kids were born back in the late fifties and early sixties.

I'd be a pretty good husband early in the labor. I'd sit by my wife's bed and when she'd have a contraction I'd say comforting things like "Uh oh" and "Look out" and "I'm feeling a little queasy now." When she'd go into the delivery room to deliver, I'd go into the waiting room to wait. I'd smoke cigarettes, look at my watch, and read *Life* magazine.

Boys in my hometown were brought up to believe this division of labor had been pretty clearly laid out in Genesis when God came down to sentence Adam and Eve for eating the apple. The deal was, you remember, that Eve had to bring forth children in sorrow and let her husband rule her. Adam had to put up with thorns and thistles, and eat bread while he had sweat on his face.

If a girl back in my hometown had asked a boy for a little help in bringing forth this child in sorrow, he'd probably have said he had to go mess with his John Deere so he could plow under those thorns and thistles and work up a sweat before lunch.

Most of us boys had the notion that God, being a Boy Himself, knew that we were too sensitive to be inside the delivery room while our children were being born. We liked to talk about the miracle of birth, but only after the baby had been washed off and wrapped up in a little pink or blue blanket and handed to us so we could chuck it under the chin and say "Hey there. Hey."

And we knew that even though Genesis was a little vague about baby showers, they were clearly a part of the sorrow of bringing forth children and hence not in our department. We were also too sensitive to withstand goofy baby shower games and watery coffee and jello salads and little lace doilies.

So I was surprised—this doesn't get back to my hometown, right?—when I had a good time at my daughter's baby shower. There were lots of other boys and there weren't any lace doilies or jello salads. We had beer and crackers and cheese and dip and chips and hot salsa and brownies, and we didn't play any games. One girl said we were going to play Pin the Diaper on the Grandpa, but it was just a joke. I laughed a little myself, but I stayed alert. Still, I was glad to be there.

My son tells me he was also glad to be in the birthing room when Lovely Little Leslie Jo was born. It's all pretty perplexing to someone with my background, but my wife tells me if my brain cells hold out I can get over knowing the things I knew while I was growing up. If I don't, she says, I can take my patriarchal notions of Divine Intent and stick them in the exhaust pipe of the John Deere I'll be messing with after she puts me out to pasture in the middle of a whole lot of thorns and thistles.

Women's History

MARCH 25, 1991

March is Women's History Month and I suppose some men are whining about it. "When do we get Men's History Month?" some of them are probably saying. But you don't hear me asking questions like that. Women's history is important to me because I'm so sensitive to all women's issues that my friends can hardly stand me. I've so thoroughly transcended the patriarchal model of marriage that I make Alan Alda look like Archie Bunker. I'm a high profile liberated male. You want evidence?

I cook.

It's a big job, especially when we have people over for a meal. My wife follows me around the kitchen, cleaning up the tomato sauce I spill into the electric clock on the stove, scouring the inside of the pan where the lasagna noodles stick, scraping up the mozzarella crumbs I drop on the electric burners.

"What a lovely lasagna," our guests tell my wife. I duck my head and dig my toe into the carpet and wait for her to say, as she always does, "I didn't do it. He did."

Then I'm wonderfully modest while my male friends squirm and my female friends look at my wife with what I choose to call envy—even though I once heard one of them whisper to her, "You poor thing."

I've been doing the cooking ever since she became an elementary school librarian. It seemed like the fair thing to do. She spends all day riding herd on hordes of kids with leaky plumbing. Oh, I put in eight-hour days too: two hours in class, maybe three more reading and writing, an hour in jovial companionship with my colleagues in committee meetings or having coffee, perhaps an hour working out and showering in our gym, and an hour or so contemplating my navel and the pleasant scene outside my office window.

We both come home from work about the same time, I whistling, she glassy-eyed and shellshocked.

"I made a really insightful comment about Thoreau today," I say. "Let me tell you about it."

"I've had 120 little kids stuck to me since 10 a.m.," she says. "They're lovely and sweet, but they wipe their noses on me and crawl into my lap and wet their pants. I don't want insights. I want comfort."

So I fix supper and feel virtuous. Later in the evening, she cleans up after me in the kitchen and washes a load of laundry and irons some clothes while I watch something ennobling on PBS and think about what I can cook the next time we have guests.

Because I like to cook. I like to buy groceries and chop them up and mix them together and smell them and cook them and watch people eat them. And I especially like having people say to my wife "That's a great stir-fry," and having her say "I didn't do it. He did."

That's high profile liberated. Low profile liberated is what my son-in-law is. He does the laundry at their house and if my daughter runs out of clean underwear, she wears his. He doesn't want anyone to know this.

The question of who does the laundry in our house doesn't come up when we have guests. Nobody says to me, "That's a nicely ironed blouse your wife is wearing. What kind of starch did you use?" And nobody asks me what I use to clean the windows or how I get the dog hair off the furniture. Nobody compliments me on how promptly the bills get paid or how neatly the checkbook balances.

If they did, I'd have to say "I didn't do it. She did."

I tell myself we divide the household duties along lines determined by what each of us likes to do—or at least by what we can't stand leaving undone. And I can stand leaving lots undone. She's genetically unable to tolerate a messy house and unpaid bills, so she takes care of those things.

She likes doing yard work—planting tulip bulbs on her hands and knees, digging weeds out of her marigolds, pruning the honeysuckle. But she doesn't have much time for that after the laundry and the bills and the tomato sauce in the electric clock.

Outsiders watching all that might conclude the bottom line in our division of labor is this: I do the work I want to do and she does the rest. They might also conclude that I'm not as liberated from the patriarchal marriage as I think I am.

But high profile liberated males are always looking for new ways of being liberated that will be noticed. In observance of Women's History Month, for example, I'm taking lessons in Male Humility and the Operation of a Toilet Bowl Brush. Now I'm waiting for someone to say "That's an exhilaratingly clean toilet bowl. Who did it?"

Looking back on her own personal woman's history, my wife says I may have a long wait.

Braumeister

JULY 16, 1990

"I suppose," I say, "we should stop and tell them about the sugar in the bottom of the bottles."

My wife and I are driving past the new Budweiser plant just off I-25 a few miles north of Ft. Collins. Even on vacation in Colorado, my mind functions in the masculine practical mode.

"They probably already know about the sugar in the bottom of the bottles," she says. "And they probably know how to read recipes. They probably even know the difference between a teaspoon and a tablespoon."

It's been nearly 30 years now, but neither of us has forgotten what I refer to as "that little trouble in the basement" and what she calls "another tightwad scheme that almost killed us all." What we're talking about is this:

We are eating breakfast in our kitchen when the explosion from the basement rattles our coffee cups. My wife's maternal logic takes her to the babies' room while I spill my orange juice and drop my toast, strawberry jam side down.

We go to the head of the basement stairs, my wife still in her robe and slippers, I in my 1961 English teacher's uniform: inch-wide tie, white shirt, flannel pants, tweed jacket with leather elbow patches, two red ballpoints beside the pack of Marlboros sticking out my left breast pocket. The Marlboros show my students that even though I teach poetry, I'm not a wimp.

"It's probably the gas furnace," I explain in my competent-male voice. "It's probably blown up. Or at least the hot water heater. Sometimes they blow up too."

But it's not the furnace and it's not the hot water heater. It's the homebrew. Sixteen quart bottles of homemade beer that we filled and capped and stored in a cardboard box day before yesterday, all sixteen touching one another so that when they explode there will be only one big boom instead of sixteen little ones.

The basement smells of something gone bad. It is one room, twenty by thirty feet, and the whole floor is covered with the sticky homebrew and pieces of glass no bigger than a dime, but sharper. Shards of it still dripping foam are imbedded in the bare floor joists overhead.

"Hey, look," I say. "The beer blew up."

My wife gives me a look like she thinks maybe I think I'm Dick Tracy and she's Tess Trueheart.

She doesn't like homebrew even when it doesn't blow up. She doesn't like its scummy look and funky smell while it's fermenting in the big clay pickle crock I found at Goodwill, and she doesn't like the taste of sucking it through the rubber tube we use to siphon it into the quart bottles she's just washed the dead flies out of.

"Think of the money we'll save," I'd said while we were filling the bottles. "This stuff is costing us about four cents a quart."

"That's about a nickle a quart more than it's worth," she'd calculated as she wiped off her chin.

Now she just looks at the glass shards imbedded in the joists and she doesn't say anything.

What went wrong, I'll later figure out when I re-read the recipe, was that I'd put too much sugar in the bottom of each bottle before we'd filled it. The sugar was to give the yeast something to feed on after the bottle had been capped so that the beer would be fizzy when we opened it.

I'd put in a tablespoon instead of a teaspoon.

We sweep up the glass. It cuts into my rubber heels and crunches under my leather soles as it grinds into the concrete floor. Then we mop up the beer. I'm going to be late for class, but I know enough to help out anyway and not say anything. Upstairs, the babies are awake and yelling. My wife speaks.

"You're a pretty good husband," she says, "but don't you ever, don't you ever make beer again."

"You know what?" I say, sucking on the finger I've just cut from picking a piece of glass out of the joist. "This is just too goshdarned much trouble. I don't think I'll ever make beer again."

I haven't either. But every time I pass a brewery, I wonder if I should stop and tell them it's a teaspoon, not a tablespoon. Driving down I-25 a couple of miles north of Ft. Collins, my wife gives me that look so I decide the hell with it. Let the Budweiser people learn in the school of hard knocks the way all of us Marlboro men did.

Whose Omelet? Whose Eggs?

NOVEMBER 19, 1990

On the day the President decides to send another 200,000 Americans to Saudi Arabia, a disk jockey on the radio says now we're ready "to kick some butt" to get the Iraqis out of Kuwait.

"Yeah," I say. "Let's kick some butt."

"The old testosterone rising?" my wife asks. "Sounds like it might be interfering with your thought processes. Better have the doctor check that out when you go in for the cholesterol test."

"I suppose you've got other smart-alecky and unpatriotic things to say."

She smiles like the Mona Lisa.

"Oh no," she says. "I'm thrilled. It makes me all quivery with manifest destiny."

"Good," I say. "People who criticize the President in times like these are just lending aid and comfort to the enemy. I'm glad you've come aboard."

"There's only one thing," she says. "I think it's time we had a military draft again."

"Wait a minute," I say. "What about our kids? You want them to go off to the desert to get shot at?"

"Don't worry," she says. "Under my plan, our kids wouldn't be eligible. Only the sons and daughters of government officials would be drafted."

"Silliest thing I ever heard of," I say. "Why do you think they'd make better soldiers than the sons and daughters of the rest of us?"

"Oh I don't," she says. "They'd probably make worse soldiers. But that's not my point."

I furrow my brow. I don't get it.

"You're furrowing your brow again. You don't get it, do you? Listen carefully: if all the sons and daughters of government officials were in the military, how often do you think they'd get sent to some desert where they might have to fight against tanks and planes and anthrax and botulism toxins?"

"Hah?" I say.

"Suppose," she says, "you were President and you knew that our three kids would be in the first wave of soldiers you were sending into Kuwait. Would that change anything?"

"Golly," I say. "I wouldn't send my kids there."

"But you'd send other people's kids where you wouldn't send your own?" she asks.

"Well, we can't be a helpless giant," I say. "We've got to have a military posture astride the oil fields."

"Only if you'd be willing to send your own kids," she says. "I'd make it a constitutional requirement: If you don't have draft-age kids, you're not eligible to run for office."

I scratch my head. I furrow my brow.

"But that wouldn't be patriotic," I say. "Would it?"

"What could be more patriotic?" she says. "What could be more in the national interest than to ask no more of any citizen than you'd ask of your own kids? We might *really* be a kinder, gentler nation then."

"But I thought patriotism was the disk jockey," I say. "The guy that's ready to kick some butt."

"Wanting to kick butt is what gives patriotism a bad name," she says. "And when I hear that kind of talk I begin to understand what Thoreau meant when he said patriotism is a maggot in our heads."

"But haven't you had it with Saddam Hussein?" I ask. "Aren't you fed up?"

"I'm fed up with anyone who uses other people's kids to act out their own frustrations," she says. "I've had it with the guy who wants to put other people's kids where his mouth is."

"When you talk that way," I say, "you're giving aid and comfort to the enemy. Aren't you?"

"When you talk that way," she says, "you've got a maggot in your head. Don't you?"

"Hah?" I say. I put my finger in my ear. She's wrong again. There's nothing there.

"You don't understand patriotic sacrifice," I say, putting on my Ollie North face; it's important to get the last word in these arguments. "After all, you can't make an omelet without breaking eggs."

"Whose omelet?" she says. "Whose eggs?"

Bread Machine

FEBRUARY 1, 1993

When male idealism and devotion to duty come up against female pragmatism, it's no contest. The apples were just hanging there and it had been a while since breakfast, so Eve did eat thereof, divine injunction be damned.

"Here," she said to Adam, licking her lips. "You have one too."

What I really wanted for my birthday, of course, was one of those nifty little gadgets that clip hair out of the inside of your nose. The Nifty Little Gadget mail-order catalogues around our house are full of them. You stick one up your nostril, push a button, and voila! no more nose hair. One of the catalogues said their deluxe model will even work on ear hair if you stick it in your ear.

"You want something that silly," my wife says, "you send off for it yourself. I don't want my name on the order. How about a nice bread-making machine?"

"The nose-hair gadget is only $6.99 plus postage," I say. "Bread machines cost more."

"We'll take it out of my half of the joint account," she says. "Don't be such a tightwad."

"You're the one," I say, "who claims you can't always tell if my nose hair is growing into my mustache or if my mustache is growing into my nose. One of these little gadgets would make me a lot more kempt."

She snorts. She doesn't have hair growing out of her nose and she doesn't understand the heartbreak of hairy ears.

She doesn't understand cause and effect either. She likes it when the house fills up with the smell of baking bread, but she doesn't understand why I have to get flour in all the kitchen drawers to make the smell.

"What in the world's going on?" she says when she comes home and catches me making bread. "It looks like ten pounds of flour in a five-pound sack in here."

"I'm worshipping at the altar of Ceres, goddess of grain," I explain. "I'm getting in harmony with my glutens. I'm making bread."

"There's flour in all the drawers," she says, "and you've got bread dough stuck to your nose hair. Or mustache. Whichever it is."

"You can't make an omelet without breaking an egg or two," I say, "and you can't make bread without getting flour in a drawer or two. Feel these glutens."

I whang the dough onto the bread board in front of her and she disappears in a cloud of flour.

"You're getting a bread machine for your birthday," she says when she reappears, "whether you want it or not."

"I want a nose-hair clipper," I say, "and I ought to get what I want. It's my birthday."

"That's not what you used to tell the kids," she says. "Gifts should reflect the values of the giver not the givee, you told them. Then you'd give them a book on the Brooklyn Dodgers."

"Cultural literacy," I say. "I had a parental obligation to get them in touch with the icons of our civilization. But bread machines are decadent. They're for yuppies. I'm no yuppie."

"Nobody's going to mistake you for one," she says. "Yuppies don't have hair growing out their ears."

So on my birthday, I get a bread machine.

"Surprise!" she says.

It's made by a Japanese electronics company and the owner's manual is published by the Tower of Babel Press. It has sentences like "It is recommended that the amount of bread flour is measured by weight method. The measuring cup is just reference for bread flour." But the pictures show me how to put all the ingredients into the little box inside the big box, then set the timer so the bread will be ready by breakfast.

I keep waking up during that first night listening to the little grunty noises the machine makes as it kneads the dough—a noise that reminds me I'm not living up to my Baptist work ethic. About 4 a.m. I fall into a guilt-ridden sleep and have a dream vision. Ceres is in it, dressed in a costume that makes her look like a loaf of cracked wheat.

"Kneadst thou thine own glutens in the sweat of thy face," she says, wagging a floury finger at me and speaking King James English. "Let not thy bread-machine kneadst them or thy yeast shalt surely stink in thy nostrils and thy crust crumble into little bitty crumbs."

She says it from inside the Mt. Olympus Bakery and Deli where they make the food for the gods. It smells heavenly.

And it's the smell that wakes me up. That part is no dream. Our house is full of it.

My temptress wife is already in the kitchen with a pot of coffee and the brand new loaf of crusty bread. She's halfway through the first slice, a little butter and strawberry jam stuck to the corner of her mouth. She pours me a cup of coffee, puts butter and jam on a second slice, and hands it to me.

"Here, you hairy-eared rascal," she says, licking her lips. "You have some too."

What Would PeeWee Reese Do?

MARCH 14, 1994

When Senate Majority Leader George Mitchell, D-Maine, says he doesn't want to be a senator anymore but he wouldn't mind being baseball commissioner, I understand. We're of the same generation.

As commissioner, he could decree that players wear baggy pants again, that the Dodgers move back to Brooklyn, that no one get a higher salary than Willie Mays got, that box seats cost $3.50, and that beer not be sold to bozos—only to genteel folk like you and me.

That is, he could re-establish major league baseball as the Great Moral Influence it used to be.

You want evidence it used to be a Great Moral Influence? Listen.

It is a Saturday in early September, 1949. I am 15 years old and, for the first time in my life, I have learned something useful. I am on my way to the barber shop to make use of it.

We get our baseball over the radio in 1949, most of it from Gordon McLendon of the Liberty Broadcasting System somewhere in Texas. What I have just learned—from the *Time* magazine that came this morning—is that by using recordings of crowd noises and a gadget that sounds like a bat hitting a ball, McLendon "recreates" games from a teletype machine that reports only the bare bones of what's happening inning by inning. What else I learn is that the recreated game runs 45 minutes behind the real one.

I finish the *Time* story and go to the shortwave band on our huge Zenith floor model radio. Sure enough, I hear through the static and electronic squeals Red Barber's voice on an overseas broadcast and he's in the second inning of the Dodger-Cardinal game that McLendon won't begin to recreate for another 15 minutes. I listen until Gil Hodges hits a three-run homer in the bottom of the ninth to win it for the Dodgers.

And here's what Satan hisses in my ear: if I get to the barber shop while McLendon is still recreating the game that I already know the outcome of, I'll have an advantage. I can hardly believe how clever I'm about to be.

It's the top of McLendon's ninth when I get there, and Ben Black, the barber, is still chortling because Stan Musial just doubled in two runs off Big Newk to put the Cards ahead 4-2 going into the bottom of the ninth.

"That's one thing about the Bums you can count on," he says. "They always choke in the tight ones. That's why they're the Bums."

I like the Dodgers. I don't think they're Bums at all. I say, "I bet you a nickle the Dodgers win this one."

"Just a nickle?" Ben says. "A real Dodger fan would bet more than a nickle. How about a dime?"

"OK," I say, my voice cracking. "How about a quarter?"

People waiting for shaves and haircuts look up, interested, while Ben and I put our quarters on the shelf next to the Bay Rum. Harry Brecheen strikes out Billy Cox just like I knew he would.

"He'll probably walk the Duke," I say, and Ben looks funny when Snider walks on a 3-1 pitch. But he's grinning again when Robinson fouls out. Now it's Campanella up with two outs.

"Brecheen's getting tired," I say. "He'll probably walk Campy too."

And, of course, that's what happens. Ben frowns. Hodges is up.

"Look at the arms on this guy," McLendon says from his Texas studio. "He could go bear hunting with a stick."

"Yeah, but he can't touch Brecheen's curve," Ben says. "It's over."

"It's over all right," I say, louder than I intend to. I'm about to wet my pants. "Big Gil's gonna plant one in the seats. Big Gil's gonna hit a home run and the Dodgers are gonna win."

"In a pig's eye," Ben says.

Hodges takes two called strikes and I have a moment of doubt. Is that the way it was on the short wave? Was *Time* telling the truth?

"In a pig's eye Hodges is even gonna touch the ball," Ben says.

He says it just before McLendon makes a hellacious bat crack and turns up the crowd noise as loud as it will go and starts screaming: "It's a long drive to left! It's going! It's going! It's gone! The Bums win!"

Ben's customers are slack-jawed and glassy-eyed. I grin. Ben hands me the quarters, but he's not grinning. He's looking hard at me—like maybe I've just made a pact with the devil.

And that's when it hits me just how wicked I'm being. Here I am, making money on a crooked bet involving the National Pastime. It's like betting with a Baptist on which rosary bead will turn up next. Sacrilege.

So I ask myself the question I always ask when I'm in a moral dilemma: What would PeeWee Reese do?

I know the answer already so I give back Ben's quarter and tell everybody about McLendon's studio in Texas and the crowd noise machine and how the real game ended 45 minutes ago.

That's what baseball was like when Sen. Mitchell and I were in our formative years. If it'd been a football game, I'd have made a killing.

Warming the Cave

NOVEMBER 5, 1990

On chilly nights now, I light a fire in our woodburning stove and feel warm and self-reliant.

"See how warm and self-reliant we are?" I ask my wife. "Minnegasco and LES can eat their hearts out."

But it hasn't always been this easy.

It is 1964 and we finally have a house of our own and I can no longer control my lust for fire.

"We'll get one of those free-standing fireplaces," I tell my wife and kids. "We'll put it in the basement and build fires in it. We'll have fun. We'll get warm. We'll roast weenies."

My wife rolls her eyes and my kids start crying.

"Hush," she tells them. "It's just Daddy's pyromania acting up again. He'll be all right after he burns something."

I go to Wards and buy a $130 stove on sale for $99, then I pick up stovepipe at a furnace place. They tell me it won't draw unless I get the chimney higher than the roof, but I know they're just trying to sell stovepipe. They say I need 25 feet, but I wasn't born yesterday. I buy five feet.

"Shouldn't you get somebody to install this?" my wife says. "Somebody who knows what he's doing?"

"Self-reliance," I say. "Cavemen built their own fires."

The kids start crying again and my wife rolls her eyes.

"I think I'll take a walk," she says. "But I'll leave the kids to help you."

So my five-year-old son and I unpack the stove while my three-year-old daughter whimpers and holds her blanket to her face.

"Now," I say, "the first thing we need is a hole for the chimney pipe. So the fire will be inside and the smoke will be outside."

I get a hammer and break out one of the panes in the basement window. My son looks worried and my daughter says, "I'm gonna tell."

I cut a piece of masonite the size of the broken pane, put a hole in it for the chimney pipe to fit through, and wedge it into the opening where the glass was. The pipe sticks out the window maybe a foot.

"That'll do," I tell the kids. "Smoke wants to go up."

My son looks dubious and my daughter says again, "I'm gonna tell."

By this time, my wife is back from her walk. My daughter tells.

"You broke a window?" my wife asks.

"To let the smoke out," I say.

"Oh," she says. "Good thinking."

We gather fallen twigs and branches from the yard and I wad up newspaper and put it in the stove with the twigs on top.

"Here we go," I say, striking a match. "Gonna warm up this cave."

The paper catches and the twigs begin to burn, but the smoke doesn't go up the pipe. It comes out the front of the stove.

"The smoke," my wife says, "is staying in the house."

"The pipe just needs to get hot so it will draw," I say. "It'll be all right. Now we'll put in some bigger wood. Then we'll roast weenies."

But the smoke keeps coming out the front.

"That's funny," I say. "It's supposed to go up."

"It isn't funny," my wife says, "and it is going up." She points to the stairway.

"Probably we just need a hotter fire," I say. "We'll put more wood on. Then it'll draw. It'll be all right. We'll have fun."

By now, we're coughing and our eyes are watering. I'm squatting by the fire, putting more wood on.

"Look," I say. "If you squat down like this, you get under the smoke. It's not so bad."

My wife and kids squat down beside me. The smoke is rolling up the stairs into the kitchen and living room and bathroom and bedrooms. We hunker closer to the floor.

"Tell me again," my wife says. "Why are we doing this?"

"Because," I say, wiping my eyes, "it's fun."

"No," she says. "This is not fun. This is crazy. This is a house, not a cave, and it's full of smoke."

"I'll get the weenies," I say, and I stand up and feel my way along the wall to the stair. My wife and kids follow me up.

"Don't go back down there," she tells the kids. "Ever."

She opens all the windows and doors. In a couple of hours, the fire dies out and by bedtime most of the smoke is gone.

"It's cold in here," I say. "Isn't it?"

"Yes," she says, "and it smells like a Neanderthal fire sale. The kids smell like little slabs of bacon. You're a pretty good husband but you've ruined the curtains and you smell like a smoked turkey."

"I'm cold," I say.

"I wanna weenie," my son says.

"I'm gonna tell grandma," my daughter says.

Christmas, 1946

DECEMBER 21, 1992

We don't have great expectations for our dogs in the little western Kansas town where I'm growing up in the 1940s.

That's why we never buy them dog food. They survive mainly on table scraps, an occasional rabbit, and a bone now and then from Darby Dunn after he's cut up the meat at Dunn's Grocery.

And when we go out of town—even at Christmas—our dogs are on their own. If they can't pull through on roadkill and the neighbors' garbage, if they can't dodge the pickups they share our gravel streets with, it simply reinforces our strong sense of canine mortality.

Mine has been formed by a sequence of dog disasters: Duke had to be summarily executed because he killed, without malice, 23 of our neighbor's baby chicks; Meatball died of worms; and we ran over a new puppy in our driveway even before we had time to name him.

We were on our way to an Abbott and Costello movie, and we went anyway.

So I'm not looking for another dog when Bully comes to live with us. He just shows up one day when I'm in fifth grade. His ribs are sticking out so my mother gives him the leftover ham and beans and cornbread she's about to throw out to the neighbor's chickens anyway.

We ask around, but nobody knows who Bully belongs to. Travelers, maybe, passing through on Highway 54, who forgot they let him out of the car when they stopped for gas.

We end up letting him hang around. We never call him our dog, but after a month I sneak him into my room at night so he can sleep at the foot of my bed.

Pretty ugly dog, mainly Boston Terrier and who knows what else. He likes to roll on dead things too, so he's usually pretty ripe. But he's lavishly grateful for the hospitality. When I come home from school, he howls and yowls in what I first think is agony but later decide is ecstasy. He makes a noise like "A-roo-roo-roo."

And he follows me around on my paper route, peeing on any tree that looks like it needs it. Our barber claims Bully saved the town's Siberian elms during the summer drought of 1946; he proposes a commemorative fountain on Main Street, a bronze of Bully lifting his leg.

Then he laughs. It's a joke.

"Don't get too attached to him," my mother tells me. "You don't have good luck with dogs."

"Yes," I sigh, looking off into the distance. "I know."

I've seen movies. I know the way tragic characters look and talk.

So when my parents decide we'll spend Christmas of 1946 on my grandparents' farm 220 miles away, I figure that's the end for Bully. During our four-day absence, he'll freeze, starve, and be run over by pickups.

"We'll leave the garage door open," my mother says. "And he can eat the Hofferbers' scraps. He'll be all right."

"Sure he will," I say, looking off into the distance and knowing what I know.

When we drive away on the afternoon of the 21st, Bully chases us the four blocks to the city limits.

My father tries to cheer me up during the four-and-a-half-hour trip.

"Look," he says when we go through towns with N-O-E-L spelled out in big tinselly letters arching over the street. "They knew we were coming and they tried to spell your name but they got it backwards."

Then he laughs. It's a joke.

I try to smile, but I know that Bully is at that moment still chasing our car down Highway 54, about to starve and freeze and be run over by a Mack truck. The best I can imagine is his showing up at my grandparents' farm, bloody pawed and whining, on Christmas morning. I'll go to the door to see who's there and he'll drop dead right in front of me.

But nothing is there when I look out the door on Christmas morning. I stare off into the distance.

"What in the world is wrong with that boy?" I hear my grandmother ask my father. "Does he have the stigmatism? Does he need cod-liver oil? Doesn't he like Christmas?"

We have to stay for Christmas supper, so we don't leave until after 7. It's a cold, clear night, lots of stars bright in the western Kansas sky, and we listen to Christmas songs on KGNO on the way home. Just before I zonk off into a deep and dreamless sleep in the backseat, I wonder if the ground will be too frozen to dig the hole when we get there.

I wake up as we turn into our driveway. The radio finishes "It Came Upon the Midnight Clear" and I get out to look for the body.

That's when something ripe and fat with garbage—a howling, yowling epiphany—comes barreling out the garage door and knocks me down, filling my nostrils with the sweet stink of dog breath. It makes a noise like "A-roo," then "A-roo-roo-roo," and just before my father turns off the ignition, the car radio instructs me to hark the herald angels sing.

My resistance gone at last, I give up. I hark.

Pinko TV

JANUARY 30, 1995

"Who's the big guy?" I ask my wife. She's watching TV. A big guy is singing.

"Hush," she says. "Pavarotti. You know. The tenor."

"Sounds like he's just off the boat," I say. "His English isn't so good, is it? If he can't sing better English than that, he ought to go back where he came from."

"He's not trying to sing English," she says. "He's singing Italian because it's an Italian opera."

Then it dawns on me. My wife is watching PBS. That's why O. J. isn't on.

"Why are you watching left-wing TV?" I say. "Why are you rotting your brain with pinko programming?"

"Have you been listening to Rush Limbaugh again?" she asks.

"It's right here in the Sunday paper," I say. "Cal Thomas says PBS 'promotes left-wing and one-sided views.' Says it's 'trashing traditional values and promoting the supposed joys of a Socialist society.' Whaddya say to that?"

"What in the world is left-wing about Pavarotti singing in Italian?" she says.

"Undermines our free-market system, that's all," I say. "Italians have socialized medicine, don't they?"

"Everybody in Europe has socialized medicine," she says. "They're civilized."

"Well, that's their problem," I say. "We shouldn't listen to their show tunes unless they admit we've got the best medical system in the world."

After Pavarotti finishes, it's Louis Rukeyser on "Wall Street Week."

"Another PBS left-wing program," my wife says. "Better not watch. It'll undermine your entrepreneurship."

"Look at him," I say. "See him arch his eyebrow when he mentions Wall Street? He's ridiculing capitalism. And those willing dupes at PBS let him do it."

Then it's the McLaughlin Group.

"McLaughlin's a really rabid pinko, isn't he?" she says. "Yet more promotion of the supposed joys of socialism. Shall I tie you to the mast and plug your ears?"

"Is that some new kinky perversion that PBS is pushing?" I ask. "I'm just glad the children aren't here. I just hope they're watching commercial TV so the grandbabies won't be corrupted."

Then it's Lawrence Welk.

"A little left-wing polka?" she says. "Insidious rascals, aren't they?"

After that, it's a Nova show on ants (thinly disguised advocacy of non-competitive, collectivist cultures), a P. G. Wodehouse Jeeves-and-Wooster story (subtly pimping for a classless society), a "Victory at Sea" rerun suggesting we were actually allies with the Russians in WWII, and a woman's basketball game played by females who should be home tending babies.

"Well," I say, "I guess you can see now what Cal Thomas means. Heh?"

"If you think that's left-wing programming," she says, "you're a troubled aging male."

"Oh yeah?" I say, my massive powers of cause-effect coming into play. "If it's not left-wing programming, why is Newt Gingrich trying to zero out its funding?"

"Cognitive dissonance," she says. "He's trying to believe two contradictory ideas at the same time. It's dangerous and Newt knows it. Too much cognitive dissonance and your synapses sizzle, sparks shoot out your ears, and you blow a fuse. So he's got to get rid of PBS."

"Huh?" I say.

"Newt's a free market true believer," she says. "His gospel is that the invisible hand of unregulated competition always, without fail, produces the best possible product. But he watches free-market TV and sees crap."

"Crap's what the consumers want," I say, but it doesn't sound right when I say it.

"Not all consumers," she says. "Even Newt, despite his gospel, knows that McNeil/Lehrer is a better news show than Chung/Rather. Twice as long, three times as balanced, ten times as informative. And McNeil/Lehrer didn't trick Newt's mama into saying what Newt called Hillary. But McNeil/Lehrer isn't free-market TV and Chung/Rather is. So there it is. Cognitive dissonance. If Newt doesn't cut off PBS funding, he'll have to stop believing in his invisible-hand gospel —or he'll blow a fuse."

"But PBS wastes tax money," I say, shifting to more familiar ground.

"Costs $1.09 per person per year," she says.

"Well," I say, "$1.09 here and $1.09 there—it adds up."

"Less than half a percent of what you'd pay for free market cable," she says.

That's the argument that finally does me in.

"OK," I say. "I'll admit that PBS is the best TV if you'll admit that the invisible hand of the free market ne'er betrayed the heart that loved it."

"You still have trouble with the cognitive dissonance concept," she says, "don't you?"

Then my synapses sizzle, sparks shoot out my ears, and, just before I blow a fuse, I think about running for Congress.

Gracious Submission

JULY 13, 1998

I was reading the paper last month and it made me say "Hah!"

"That's your exclamation-point hah indicating a bias has been reinforced," my wife said, "as opposed to your question-mark hah indicating greater-than-usual befuddlement."

"Hah?" I said.

"So which bias is it?" she asked.

"Check this out," I said, holding up a story headlined "Baptists say men should lead couples."

It was all about how the Southern Baptist Convention amended its Statement of Belief by adding that a husband should "lead his family," and that a wife should "submit herself graciously."

"Let's give it a try," I said. "For the next month, I lead, and you submit yourself graciously. OK?"

"Whatever," she said, going back to her crossword puzzle. "What's a six-letter Greek word for overweening pride and arrogance?"

So we've been trying the Southern Baptist formula for the last month. We still have a few bugs to work out.

I'm quite good, I must say, at leading my wife. And she at least goes through the motions of submitting.

But we're hung up on the "graciously" part.

I began by training her to walk three or four paces behind me when we were out in public. She submitted, but kept asking if she couldn't make it 15 or 20 paces so no one would know we were together. People heard.

When I told her to stop getting my attention by saying "Hey, Bozo," she began saying "Heigh-de-ho, Lord and Master," and "Yo, Big Enchilada," and "Whazzup, Your Blinding Magnificence."

I particularly liked that last one. And spoken in the proper tone of voice, it might be considered an act of gracious submission. But it loses something when accompanied by snorts, eye-rollings, and gagging noises.

"Look," I tell her, "it's been a month now, and your submission seems to grow less gracious by the day. In fact, it seems to be coarse mockery—and thereby an affront both to me and to the Southern Baptist Convention."

"So why, O Light o' My Life," she says, "are you so hot to follow the Southern Baptists in this little exercise in pious sexism?"

"I'm following the power," I say. "Bill Clinton, Al Gore, Trent Lott, Newt Gingrich—they're all Southern Baptists and look where it got them."

She looks as though she's just sniffed an offensive emission.

"Power through misogyny?" she says.

"It's not misogyny," I say. "Listen to this."

And I read her the part of the revised Statement of Belief that says "The husband and the wife are of equal worth before God."

"If we're of equal worth," she says, "why do you get to lead while I get to submit graciously? What's equal about that?"

"It's an analogy," I explain. "Listen to this."

And I read her the part of the statement that says "A wife is to submit graciously to the servant leadership of her husband even as the church willingly submits to the headship of Christ."

"Internal contradiction," she says.

"Hah?" I say.

"If the analogy is that you're Christ and I'm the church, we're not equal," she says. "Baptists would never say the church is equal to Christ. If they really mean that husband and wife are equal, they should say that whichever one is most Christ-like gets to lead and the other one has to submit graciously. To tie Christ-like qualities to the Y chromosome is blasphemously reductionist, wouldn't you say?"

"Play fair," I say. "You can't speak in big words and long paragraphs in this column. Besides, you ignore the scriptural authority."

And I whip out my New Testament and quote from Paul's letter to the Ephesians: "Wives, submit yourselves unto your own husbands, as unto the Lord. For the husband is the head of the wife, even as Christ is the head of the church."

"But that's Paul talking, not Christ," she says. "When Paul talks about women, he's about as divinely inspired as Archie Bunker."

If there's one thing the family head can't tolerate, it's an uppity wife arguing with scripture. I put my foot down.

"Stifle, Dingbat," I say in my Charlton Heston voice. "Submit thyself graciously to My Blinding Magnificence or, hoo boy, are you gonna be sorry."

She smiles sweetly, sticks out her tongue in a Bronx cheer, thumbs her nose, makes a rude gesture, and says "Submit this."

"Hah?" I say, feeling a tectonic power shift rumbling down deep in the nether regions of inter-gender theology.

I wonder if I should alert Bill, Al, Trent, and Newt.

I'd better ask my wife.

Candid Candidates

APRIL 20, 1992

It's an irony of our language that while "candid" and "candidate" are cheek by jowl in the dictionary, hardly anyone would ever think to put the two words together in any other context. We've grown to expect our politicians to rank somewhere between used car salesmen and television evangelists in letting it all hang out.

They'd be a lot more appealing—and interesting—if they'd follow the example set by our national fountainhead of intuitive wisdom, Mark Twain, back in 1879 when he decided to run for president. But first he set out to "own up in advance to all the wickedness I have done" so that voters wouldn't be shocked when his opposition pointed it out.

He admitted that "I treed a rheumatic grandfather of mine in the winter of 1850. He was old and inexpert in climbing trees, but with the heartless brutality that is characteristic of me, I ran him out of the front door in his nightshirt at the point of a shotgun, and caused him to bowl up a maple tree, where he remained all night.... I will do it again if I ever have another grandfather."

And there was more:

"I ran away at the battle of Gettysburg... because I was scared. I wanted my country saved, but I preferred to have someone else save it. I entertain that preference yet."

And still more:

"The rumor that I buried a dead aunt under my grapevine was correct. The vine needed fertilizing, my aunt had to be buried, and I dedicated her to this high purpose."

A few more admissions and Twain sat back to await the call of the people. It didn't come in his lifetime, but his tactic might have more appeal today. If we're serious when we say we've had enough of what we've got, we might vote for the absolutely candid candidate just because he'd be such a novelty.

Bill Clinton's history is pretty well known by now, thanks to the gumshoes who've been out raking his muck. Think how much more attractive his wicked past would be had he been the first to tell us about it.

"I'm Bill Clinton," we can imagine him saying back in December, "and I avoided the draft, smoked pot, appointed friends to high office, and played a little hanky-panky. I'd like your vote."

Could you resist that?

It's probably too late for Clinton to get full benefit from his wickedness—unless there's something the gumshoes haven't revealed yet. If there is, he should come out with it quick.

"I'm Bill Clinton," he could say, "and you already know about the draft, the pot, the favoritism, and the hanky-panky. But did you know I wear a wig? Did you know when Hillary's not home, I watch 'Hee Haw' reruns? I need your help."

Quick study that he is, George Bush would see voters being turned on by such revelations and he'd jump right in. There'd be a competitive frenzy of self-incrimination.

"Me?" the president might say conspiratorially. "Total depravity."

Sensing voter approval, he'd get into serious confession.

"No new taxes? Always knew there would be. Changed stance on abortion? Wherever the votes are. No center. No core. Sons rich by own merit? Own effort? Not old dad's position? Reality check."

Barbara would be giving him a look by now, but he wouldn't notice.

"Panama? Iraq? Freedom? Democracy?" he'd ask, sticking out his chin and shifting into his no-wimp voice. "Vendetta! Personal! Noriega, Saddam—big doublecross! Big payback!"

Marlin Fitzwater would edge toward the President. Secretary of State Baker would look concerned. Danny Quayle would stop grinning. The President would flail on, his voice loud and shrill now.

"Candor? Honesty? Hate it! Can't stand it! Whatever's needed for re-election! Anything! Even truth!"

The Secret Service agents would close in.

"One more thing!" he'd yell just before they grabbed him. "Clinton's wig bad? Hair dye, face lift here!"

One of them would put his hand over the President's mouth. But not before he got it all out: "Girdle! Fanny tuck!"

They'd take him away then. Just in time too. Maybe, on second thought, the nation isn't ready for George Bush to let it all hang out. Too scary. Too many secrets. Too few verbs.

Proper Presidential Age

FEBRUARY 22, 1999

"Didn't I tell you?" I say to my wife. "I told you, didn't I?"

"I suppose you did," she says, not even looking up from her crossword puzzle. "Told me what?"

"You know good and by golly well what," I say. "About Clinton."

"Oh, yes," she says, chewing on her pencil eraser. "What was it about Clinton you told me?"

"That he was a bad idea," I say. "Surely you remember me saying that Clinton was a bad idea."

"Of course," she says. "When?"

"When he ran for president," I say. "He was a bad idea when he ran for president."

"Let's see," she says, digging through her knitting basket for her little red book called Sayings of His Blinding Magnificence. "Yes, here it is. In 1992, you pointed out that Clinton was born in the Forties and we hadn't yet had a president born in the Thirties, the decade of your birth, so Clinton was a bad idea for cutting in line ahead of Depression babies. Is that what you mean?"

"Depression babies," I say, "don't care about petty things like someone cutting in line ahead of us. We're just happy we have enough lard sandwiches to eat."

"Oh," she says, and she again flips through the pages of her little red book. "Then this must be it. Just before his re-election you said Clinton was a bad idea because he didn't have neck wattles and you did. Is that it?"

"That's even sillier," I say. "No political pundit worth his unidentified sources would say Clinton's a bad idea just because he doesn't have neck wattles."

"OK," she says. "I give up. Why is Clinton a bad idea?"

"Too young," I say. "Not old enough. Only 46 when he took office."

"What's wrong with 46?" she says. "You were 46 a long, long time ago."

"Yes I was," I say. "But I had the good sense not to be president at the time."

"Quite right," she says. "Remind me. What's wrong with being president and 46 simultaneously?"

"Think about it," I say in my kind-teacher voice. "Who else was president in his 40s?"

"Let me see," she says, digging through her knitting for her World Almanac. "Polk, Pierce, Grant, Garfield, Cleveland, Teddy Roosevelt, JFK."

"Forget the first ones," I say. "They were in the Dark Ages. But look at JFK."

"OK," she says. "Now what?"

"What do you think of when you think of JFK?" I ask.

"Good looking," she says. "Pretty wife. Charming kids. Marilyn Monroe singing Happy Birthday, Mr. President."

"There!" I say. "That last one."

"Clinton got it on with Marilyn Monroe?" she says. "I didn't know that."

"Of course he didn't," I say, smiling at her charmingly anachronistic female mind. "But you're on the right trail. Elect a man in his 40s as president and he's a bad idea—because his hormones are still raging and he'll be easy pickings for any intern out there who wants to show him her thong underwear."

She gets out the little red book and scribbles something in it.

"Thank you," I say. "I'm pleased that you preserve my words for posterity."

"They'll be handy," she says, "when it's time to put you in the booby hatch."

"Hah?" I say. She's too busy rolling her eyes to answer.

"So it's like I told you," I continue. "We need to elect presidents only after they outgrow their testosterone overload. Presidents have power, and as Henry Kissinger says, power is the ultimate aphrodisiac. Anyone who combines testosterone overload with the ultimate aphrodisiac is a bad idea."

"So," she says, "it's Strom Thurmond in 2000?"

"No, m'love," I say. "Strom Thurmond is befuddled. We need a president who is in that narrow range between perpetual confusion and perpetual horniness. Somewhere in that Golden Age before wisdom turns to senility, and after the torrential rapids of giddy youth turn to gentle, sweet-flowing crystaline streams of maturity and moderation."

"Good grief," she says. "And what Golden Age might that be—in human years?"

"Oh," I say, "I'd guess somewhere between, say, 64 and 66. About."

"And how old," she asks, "might you be now?"

"As if you didn't know, dear heart," I say. "'Twas but a month ago I turned 65."

She starts digging in the knitting basket for her little red book.

"You're overlooking the obvious," she says. "If you really want a responsible president, Bozo, get a woman. Late befuddlement, early maturation."

"You jest," I say, growing pale. "The rib more mature than its source?"

"You judge," she says. "Bill or Hillary?"

"Play fair," I whimper. I'm feeling some early-onset confusion.

"Imagine this," she says. "Brad Pitt singing Happy Birthday, Ms. President."

"Hah?" I say, pulling my blanky up under my chin. "A woman president? Hah?"

"Get used to it," she says. "It's time.

I whimper more plaintively. I go into a fetal position. I put my thumb in my mouth.

She makes another entry in the little red book.

Playing Trombone

JANUARY 28, 1991

Since it didn't do any good to brood about George Bush, I've been brooding lately about Milli Vanilli. I don't need to remind you that they're the guys who lost their Grammy award when they admitted that they only moved their lips while somebody else really made all those noises.

What set me brooding was the memory of how my own musical career, like a mirror image of theirs, came to a disgraceful end: Milli Vanilli is disgraced for faking art; I was disgraced for refusing to fake it. It's a funny world.

It happens when I am a high school junior in 1951. I am a malcontent clarinet player in the school band, unhappy because I know the clarinet is not my medium. I can never pucker my chin in that tight little way good clarinetists have, and I don't like soaking my reed in my own saliva. It is esthetically unpleasing to someone as sensitively tuned to art as I am.

Artists need acclaim, or at least acceptance, and I don't get it. I've been a third clarinet for more than two years. Freshmen are recruited into the clarinet section still chewing eighth-grade bubble gum, which they sometimes get stuck between their reeds and mouthpieces, and even they move ahead of me into the second clarinets.

What I really want to play, of course, is the trombone. Every male in school wants to play the trombone, to make those wonderful trombone noises, swinging the bell up and down, sliding the slide in and out. It is the most macho instrument in the band.

Meredith Wilson hasn't written "76 Trombones" yet, but as soon as he does, all the males of my generation will vibrate.

Our school has only four trombones, so the best athletes get them. They make up the front row of our 32-piece marching band, swinging along just behind the drum majorette in her sparkly uniform and high feathered hat, and the twirlers in their short skirts and white cowboy boots with tassles. The clarinets squawk and squeal back in rows five, six, and seven.

Nobody wants to play the clarinet, but the school has twelve of them so unless you have clout or can buy your own instrument, you end up with a clarinet.

"I feel the trombone is really my medium," I tell the band director. "I mean it's the instrument I most resonate to. I saw Jack Teagarden in a movie once. Let me play the trombone. Please."

"Put on 20 pounds, grow four inches, and make the starting five on the basketball team next year," he says. "Then we'll see."

I've been to enough movies to know that lots of show biz careers get launched when someone has to fill in for someone else. So when the second trombonist (and first string quarterback) gets sick out the window of the band bus on the way to Guymon, Oklahoma for the Second Annual Panhandle Roundup Days Parade and Rodeo, I am ready to fill in.

"It'll look funny with just three trombones on the front row," the band director tells me. "You carry a trombone and act like you're playing it. It'll make the clarinets sound better too."

So there I am, marching just behind the drum majorette and the twirlers, carrying a trombone in the front row with our leading groundgainer and the two starting forwards. On "The Washington Post March" and "El Capitan," I lipsynch it the way I am supposed to, watching the other three out the corner of my eye and trying to puff out my cheeks and move my slide in and out when they do. We're still two blocks from the main downtown intersection and here there are only three grade school kids and a dachshund lining the street.

And I am still remembering the band director's last words when he handed me the trombone: "Remember, just act like you're playing it. Whatever you do, don't make any noise with it."

It sounds like censorship, I am thinking, like a violation of my first amendment rights to free expression, an affront to my artistic integrity. I'm a little light-headed.

And when we get to the center of town and there are people on both sides of the street and we strike up "Columbia the Gem of the Ocean," I go giddy in the rapture of it all. I have a chance at greatness. I have a chance to escape the third clarinet section. I have a chance to make trombone noises. It is too much to resist.

So I play the trombone. Right through the main intersection of Guymon, Oklahoma, blatting like a great flabby elephant gone flatulant, moving the slide raucously in and out, pointing the bell first at the pavement in front of me, then rakishly at the heavens above, I play the trombone. It is glorious.

It is also the Gotterdammerung end of my career. The band director says I can either quit the band or go back to soaking my reed in my own saliva with the other third clarinets, he doesn't care which, but I've blown my chance of ever playing trombone in his band. Whether I ever start a basketball game or not.

Ah, Milli! Ah, Vanilli! Ah, Art!

Cars

JANUARY 13, 1992

In *The Canterbury Tales,* Chaucer's Parson asks a rhetorical question: If gold rusts, what shall iron do? Not everyone reads it this way, but I think he's talking about cars.

Some heavy thinkers in Washington believe that most of our troubles would go away if we could just convince the rest of the world—and ourselves—that we make better cars than other countries do. That's why the head honchos from GMC, Ford, and Chrysler went with the President last week to persuade the Japanese to buy Buicks and Plymouths and Lincolns instead of Toyotas and Hondas and Subarus.

It reminds me of the arguments we used to have between the Ford men and the Chevy men in my hometown barbershop. We didn't much care which church you went to so long as you didn't get serious about your religion. But the kind of car you drove was a matter of real dispute, some of it mechanical and esthetic, most of it metaphysical and hotly held.

I think the current argument over their cars vs. ours is just about as futile.

Because the truth is that all cars, American or foreign, have but one ultimate goal and that is to break the hearts of their owners. We need to understand that so that we're not tempted to bomb Tokyo or Stuttgart or Detroit when our cars do us in. That's what they're supposed to do. That's their *raison d'etre.*

Sure, I know—we all have anecdotal evidence of automotive benevolence. We can all tell stories like the one I tell about my '76 Dodge pickup with 145,000 miles on it, a pickup that took me on a 500-mile trip in 100-degree temperatures only to blow out its right front tire just as I pulled into my own driveway.

"There," I say, "is a vehicle that's all heart, a true-blue demonstration of how the tough get going when the going gets tough, of how quitters never win and winners never quit."

And so on.

But when cars serve us well like that, they are like the mule Josh Billings wrote about: it would be a good mule for six months just to get a chance to kick somebody. For every blowout in the driveway, there are four breakdowns in the middle of Death Valley just after the dog has been car sick.

My cars have specialized in betrayals that erode family trust.

There was the '64 Mercedes 190D which overheated and warped its head. My older son, who was in high school and had thus begun to doubt his father's omniscience, helped me take off the head, get it planed, get everything back together and running again. I could see new respect in his eyes. We took it for a test run to Kansas City but 25 miles out, between Bennet and Palmyra, the oil pressure gauge dropped to zero. We opened the hood and everything was drenched with Quaker State 10-40 and a boy's faith in his father destroyed.

Or there was the '76 Honda I sold to my younger son after I was finished with it. He'd been away to college and so had begun to doubt his father's virtue. But when I let him have the car for $300 ($50 less than book retail), his eyes misted over in gratitude. His vision cleared at mile marker 413 on I-80 when the engine seized up the first time he took it out of town. He had to call me to come tow him home in the pickup, and his voice was the voice Isaac might have used to ask Abraham to explain one more time why sons should trust fathers.

And a decade earlier, there was the '66 GMC Handi-Van I had to talk my wife into buying. The engine sat inside the van between the front seats and I said it would be fun to check the oil while the kids and the dog frolicked in the back. She gave in and the van blew a head gasket in the middle of the night in the middle of Minnesota. I worked three hours at replacing it, leaning over from the driver's seat while she held the flashlight and while the kids and the dog frolicked in the back.

"Why don't we go now, Daddy?" one of the kids asked about an hour into the project.

"Shut up," I explained, stealing a line from Ring Lardner.

It didn't stay fixed. Two weeks later, it broke down in the middle of the intersection of 48th and O in the middle of July while my wife was trying to get home with my daughter's ice-cream birthday cake before it melted. That evening, my daughter said that while in some respects

I was a pretty good father, the Handi-Van and I had ruined her tenth birthday party and quite possibly the rest of her life.

But at least it was an American-built disaster.

The moral is this: Any nation that links its success to the reputation of the cars it builds is living in a Fool's Paradise. If an Infiniti rusts, what shall a Yugo do?

Puberty Revisited

MAY 22, 1995

"It's about the onset of puberty," I say, trying to maintain professorial dignity. The classroom window is open and it's May and lilac odors fill the room. We're reading e.e. cummings' poem about a world gone "mud-luscious" and "puddle-wonderful," about a "goat-footed" balloon man calling to the children to follow him because, we're told over and over, "it's spring."

"And spring," I intone, "is conventionally associated with awakening sexuality. Remember in Chaucer that old January's young wife is named May and when she gets into his garden with that pear tree. . . ."

I go on and on, my voice getting louder and louder. Some students smirk, others twitch, still others roll their eyes.

The eye-rollers agree with my wife who says that in my dotage I see the onset of puberty in everything.

"It's because of that podunk town where you grew up," she says. "Watching puberty set in was the only entertainment you had there."

"We appreciated Transcendence," I say with great dignity. "We were finely attuned to manifestations of Cosmic Benevolence."

But she's right. Puberty was the most exciting thing that happened in my hometown. We were so excited about it that we got sex mixed up with everything. Even candy bars with names like Nestlé that we couldn't pronounce.

So I am 14 in 1948 and it is a May morning and school is just out for the summer and the lilacs are in bloom and I am sitting at the drugstore soda fountain being waited on by one of the Bachman twins, either Elsie Kay or Elva May. They are 17 and identically the prettiest girls in town and, I just learned in the junior high locker room, they have reputations for being fast.

I'm not sure what that means, but I figure it has something to do with their not being Baptist and with their mother being named Belle.

I've been uneasy in the drugstore ever since I learned last month in the junior high locker room that they sell—not that I'd ever buy one—condoms under the counter. Only we can't say "condoms" in my hometown so we call them "rubbers." And that means we can't call our overshoes "rubbers" after puberty sets in. We have to call them "galoshes"—a word free of sexual associations for all but the most depraved among us.

So sitting at the soda fountain watching Elva May or Elsie Kay dip up vanilla ice cream, knowing she is fast and maybe sells condoms under the counter—it all makes me very nervous. Her blouse is open at the top maybe too far and when she leans over to dip up the vanilla ice cream you can see down to the rounded tops of her bosoms and for a second it crosses my mind that maybe she knows you can see that far and doesn't care.

And I'm remembering what one of the twins told Billy Don Hofferber just last week when he said "I wanna Baby Ruth." She laughed a little and said "Hey, Bud, my name isn't Ruth," but Billy Don is only 12 so he didn't get it.

I'm also remembering that when Bob Sturgeon, the quarterback on the football team, said he wanted an Oh Henry, Elsie Kay or Elva May just looked at him, laughed a little, and said real soft and slow "Oooooh, Henry!"

So I'm sitting at the soda fountain wondering what the twins would say if you asked for a Bit O' Honey, or even a Tootsie Roll—not that I'd ask for either. Elva May or Elsie Kay finishes dipping the vanilla ice cream and looks up to see what I'll have.

I look away from her blouse to the candy bar display behind the counter.

"I wanna Nestle," I say, pronouncing it like "wrestle."

She laughs a little and says "Well, Bud, come on back here."

"Huh?" I say.

"You wanna nestle," she says. "Come on back here, Bud, and we'll nestle."

Then I see that she is making the same kind of candy bar joke she made with Billy Don, except I am 14 and going through puberty so I get it. My face gets hot and I look at myself in the big mirror behind the counter and I am all red and I can see her back side in the mirror at the same time I can see her front side facing me and from behind I can see her skirt nipping in at her waist and from in front I can see her vanilla bosoms rising against her blouse which is open maybe further than it should be. It's more Cosmic Benevolence than I can stand.

So I panic. I leave without my candy bar.

On the way out I step on my shoestring right in front of the magazine display and nearly fall into the *True Romance* with the pouty-lipped woman on the cover.

"'Scuse me," I say, and stumble out into the May morning.

Now, 47 years later, my students and I read cummings and talk about May and lilacs and vanilla ice cream and other things Transcendent. I try to maintain professorial dignity. My voice gets louder and louder.

Christmas Discussion

DECEMBER 15, 1997

As is the custom at our house, my wife and I are observing the Christmas season with theological disputation.

"When are you going to do your Christmas shopping?" she says in her opening move, the old assertion-disguised-as-question gambit.

We have a division of labor for Christmas shopping. I buy my gift for her and any grandkid toys I might like to play with. She buys the rest: gifts for me, the kids, grandkids (toys I might not like to play with), in-laws, nephews, nieces, great nephews, great nieces, and dogs of the extended family.

So when she asks me when I'm going to do my Christmas shopping, there's a little edge in her voice. She's been shopping every day since Thanksgiving. I haven't been shopping at all. My keen senses detect danger.

"Soon," I say. "Very soon indeed. Have you made a list for me?"

"You don't make a list for me," she says. "Why should I make one for you?"

"Because, my little cottage cheese blintz," I say, "I ask you to and you are my wife. According to Paul's letter to the Ephesians 5:22, wives are to submit unto their husbands as unto the Lord."

It just slips out. Usually I'm pretty good at covering up my divinely ordained status as head honcho, but this time it just slips out. There's a perceptible stiffening of her spine.

"Poor old Paul," she says. "There he goes again."

"Meaning what, m'love?" I ask. "Nothing blasphemous, I trust."

"Meaning," she says, "that poor old Paul is once again turning his hangups about women into Scripture. So that certain unnamed boobs can use Holy Writ to justify having their wives do the Christmas shopping for them."

I duck and cover so I won't get hit by the shrapnel from the thunderbolt. But no thunderbolt comes.

"You've gone too far this time, my little sweet patootie," I say, dusting myself off. "You can't call your husband—your lord and master, your spiritual pathfinder and ethical lighthouse—a boob."

"Boob," she says. "Boob, boob, boob."

"But you're supposed to submit, honeybunch," I say. "Don't you remember that Paul says in the first letter to the Corinthians 11:3 that the head of the woman is the man?"

"O Lord," she says in a not very devotional tone, "Paul also tells the Hebrews to 'obey them that have rule over you, and submit yourselves.' He's got a thing about hierarchy and submission. He'd have us still singing 'God Save the Queen.' You don't see Jesus saying things like that."

"You don't?" I say. "Aren't they all singing from the same divine inspiration? Jesus, Paul, the Gospel guys, John the Divine, all those Old Testament dudes?"

"Not Jesus," she says. "Jesus wasn't into hierarchy. He made trouble for hierarchy. He was an agitator trying to overthrow the old order."

"Jesus Christ Superstar?" I say, my noble brow furrowed. "Where do you get that stuff?"

"The usual sources," she says. "Sermon on the Mount. Parables. The other red-letter evidence. You know why he doesn't sound like the others, don't you?"

"I suppose I don't," I say. "Why doesn't he sound like the others?"

"Different blood lines," she says. "Better gene pool."

"Hah?" I say.

"No testosterone pollution," she says. "No males involved in the production. Just an off-the-shelf woman who knew not a man, and the Holy Ghost. A man would have messed it all up with his hierarchy genes. A man would have turned the Beatitudes into the weekly power ratings. Who's number one? Who has to grovel?"

"But," I say. "But, but."

"Doesn't it seem a little strange even to your testosterone-besotted mind," she says, "that males perceive themselves anointed as family leaders by a religion whose founder was the offspring of non-testosterone carriers?"

"But," I say. "But, but."

"Sojourner Truth had it right more than a century ago," she says.

"Sojourner who?" I say.

"Sojourner Truth, and she said 'Man says woman can't have as much rights as man, cause Christ wasn't a woman. Where did your

Christ come from? From God and a woman. Man had nothing to do with him.' Put that in your patriarchal pipe and smoke it."

As if on cue, the radio bursts forth with "It Came Upon the Midnight Clear," and Ned, the one-eyed beagle with the headstrong personality and the mismatched jaws, bays in alarm.

"At least," she tells him, "you've been fixed."

When she starts to talk like that, I know the theological disputation is over and it's time for me to get out of the house for a while. I draw myself up in full patriarchal dignity, grab the car keys and hightail it to the mall to check out grandkid toys I might like to play with.

Defending Marriage

SEPTEMBER 23, 1996

"Praise God and the U.S. Congress!" I say to my Dearly Beloved as I point to the front-page story. "Blessed be the tie that binds! The institution of matrimony has been saved!"

"Oh?" she says with no visible signs of alarm at my exclamation points. "Did they pass a law requiring that husbands be certified in toilet-bowl cleaning?"

"Better than that, m'love," I say. "They passed the Defense of Marriage Act and Clinton says he'll sign it."

"Must be an election year," she says. "And just how will the Defense of Marriage Act defend marriage?"

"For one thing, my little enchilada," I say, "it defines marriage as a legal union between one man and one woman. How about that?"

"Every failed marriage I've heard of," she says, "started out as a legal union between one man and one woman. How's this going to help?"

I gently explain—in a hushed voice—that it means the feds won't recognize or give spousal benefits to gay marriages.

"But," she says, "how will that defend straight marriages?"

"Just think about it a minute, Peg o' My Heart," I say.

There's a minute of silence.

"OK," she says. "I just thought about it. I still don't get it. How's the Defense of Marriage Act going to defend marriage?"

"I won't belittle your intelligence, Snookums," I say, squirming just a little, "by belaboring the obvious."

"Go ahead," she says. "Belabor the obvious."

"Well, Honey Lips," I say, taking a deep breath, "not recognizing gay marriage defends straight marriage by keeping the institution Biblically pure."

I whip out my Bible and read aloud Leviticus 18:22 where God tells Moses "Thou shalt not lie with mankind, as with womankind: it is abomination."

She looks over my shoulder and points to Leviticus 19:19 where God tells Moses "Thou shalt not let thy cattle gender with a diverse kind: thou shalt not sow thy field with mingled seed: neither shall a garment mingled of linen and woollen come upon thee."

"If Congress is going to pass the bill because of what's in Leviticus," she says, "should it also discriminate against marriage between people who have crossbred cattle? Or hybrid corn? Or wear linen and wool together? Wouldn't that be an even stronger Biblical defense of marriage?"

I scratch my beard and look wise.

"Ah, *mein kleines Weinerschnitzel,*" I say. "Gays don't procreate. Marriage is for procreators."

"I see," she says. "So shouldn't Congress also refuse to sanction straight marriages that don't procreate? Have a baby in, say, two years or your marriage gets federally annulled. Wouldn't that be fair?"

I suck air through the gap in my front teeth and look out the window a while.

"Gay marriages, Dearie Doo," I say, "shouldn't be acknowledged because everybody knows that gays are notoriously promiscuous. They'd make a mockery of the vows."

"Good point," she says, "but shouldn't we withhold federal recognition when promiscuity sets in on straight marriages? Man steps out on wife and bingo, the FBI's on his trail and he has to pay back all the federal benefits he got for being married. That'd work, wouldn't it?"

Poor thing. She'll never learn to think like a man. I furrow my brow and try to put the argument in terms she'll understand.

"The Defense of Marriage Act defends marriage because it's pro-family, my little poppy seed muffin," I say. "We know it's pro-family because when Bob Kerrey voted against it, the Christian Coalition said he was anti-family."

"Oh well," she says. "That's settled then."

"I detect sarcasm, Small Vanilla Frozen Yogurt Cone o' Mine," I say.

"You do indeed," she says. "That's because you still haven't explained how discouraging gay marriages defends straight marriages."

I pinch the space between my eyebrows and try one more time.

"The Defense of Marriage Act does something else," I say. "It defends the heterosexual dignity of individual states by saying they don't have to honor gay marriages performed in another state. Whaddya say to that, Yum Yum?"

"I say this," she says, whipping a copy of the U.S. Constitution out from under her knitting. "Article IV, Section 1: 'Full faith and credit shall be given in each State to the public acts, records, and judicial proceedings of every other State.' Whaddya say to that, Bozo?"

I give it up then. I know better than to argue with someone who keeps a copy of the Constitution under her knitting.

And besides, "Bozo" doesn't sound like a term of endearment. Makes me think that if we talk much more about the Defense of Marriage Act, it might endanger our marriage.

Cheerleaders

AUGUST 27, 1990

This time of year I get uneasy, full of a vague sense of impending disaster, of catastrophe lurking just around the corner. And it's not just because my garden is spewing out zucchini the size of nuclear submarines or because hay fever season is about to begin.

It's because the outbreak of cheerleader season is upon us. The first football games are only days away and the dread pom-pom buds are about to burst all around us.

Spring and summer sports like track and baseball are pastoral and restful and serene—largely because there are no cheerleaders. But football season brings them out of their summer clinics full of frantic pep and the latest routines; basketball season, indoors and cramped, puts them almost literally in our laps.

That's why I sit as high in the bleachers as I can. I tell people it's because I get a better view of the whole playing field, but I'm really trying get away from the cheerleaders. From up there I can pretend not to see them.

Because cheerleaders embarrass me. When they come cartwheeling onto the field, I feel like a peeping tom and I look away.

I may as well admit it: I look on them as sex objects. I know I shouldn't say it. I know it's not very liberated, but I just can't help it. It's the way I was brought up.

I grew up in a town where we'd all have been aghast at the notion of a male cheerleader. Males were supposed to be the objects of the cheers. And only the sexiest girls became cheerleaders—on the valid assumption that it's a lot easier to produce crowd noise if you can first get the crowd's interest. The most inherently interesting subject in our town was sex.

Probably that's not the way things are in this enlightened age.

Probably nubile girls in short skirts can jump and cavort and squeal without arousing the libido of the crowd, and probably they can do it in total innocence.

If you were to ask them what they are doing, probably not many would say, "Why, sir, I am publically displaying my body in provocative stances in order to appeal to the prurient interest of the opposite sex so that they will make loud noises which the noseguard who's just had his eye gouged will interpret as support for his efforts."

Such a notion would cause most cheerleaders to collapse their pyramids in flustered indignation. They know that they're really promoting school spirit and home court advantage because that's probably what they're told at the cheerleader clinics.

But in my hometown, the cheerleaders didn't go to clinics. They made it on their sex appeal—and the boys, whether in the stands or on the team, watched and ogled. The coach would have to snap his fingers and say "Hey!" to get us out of our fantasies and back in the game. We didn't have a very good win-loss record, but that seemed secondary.

I continued to ogle cheerleaders for a couple of decades, and was happy doing it. Then my kids grew up and I was horrified one day to realize that I was ogling my daughter's classmates.

It seemed to me a bad idea that anyone in my daughter's generation should be ogled, especially when the ogler was a dirty old man like me. Then it further occured to me that every cheerleader who ever sis-boombahed was in the same generation as somebody's daughter and, more shocking, was even somebody's daughter herself.

That took the tuck right out of me.

That's when I stopped ogling and averted my eyes. That's when I started being embarrassed by cheerleaders. That's when I started to dread the beginning of cheerleader season.

Don't get me wrong. I don't object to sexual displays, to ritualized come-ons, serious or not. But I like them best when the sender and the receiver of the signal agree on what's being signified. When those displays are acted out by Girl Scouts all innocent of how they're being interpreted by dirty old men like me, I grow uneasy.

And when I remember that those kittenish bumps and grinds are coming from somebody's daughter, I squirm. I look away and wait for spring.

Saving Money

OCTOBER 24, 1994

Lots of people are making fun of the "Contract With America" that all those Republican congressional candidates signed in front of the Capitol earlier this month. The contract says if we elect them they'll reduce the deficit at the same time they cut taxes and increase spending for the Gipper's old Star Wars moneypit.

The White House calls it "Voodoo II" and says it's the same game we played in the Reagan-Bush years when the National Debt quadrupled.

But I don't make jokes about it. I like believing something so much you don't let facts get in the way.

For example, I'm still convinced I saved money by towing my '79 Rabbit home from Iowa. I scraped my shins and grated my knuckles and got sweat in my eyes. So I must have saved money. Don't confuse me with numbers.

I bought the Rabbit in the first place because it was vastly economical. It was a diesel and it was noisy and uncomfortable and stinky and hard to start in the cold, but it was the best car I ever owned. If I drove slow enough I could get more than 50 miles to the gallon.

There was a preternatural bond between me and the Rabbit. My wife said it reminded her of voodoo. Every year on my birthday, I'd take it out to see if I could match its miles per gallon with my pulse rate and my age. And every year I did. At 59, I had to drive 40 mph down Highway 6 with 23 cars and trucks honking behind me, but I got exactly 59 miles per gallon. And my pulse rate was going pocketa-pocketa at exactly 59 rpms.

My wife is too fact-haunted to understand, but I took it as a sign that my life and my vehicle were in cosmic harmony.

So I was a little reluctant to lend the Rabbit to My Son the Graduate

Student in Iowa City when his Bug expired. He said I'd get it back before my 60th birthday last winter. But it quit running when cold weather came just before Christmas.

"The Rabbit died," my son said on the telephone. "The mechanic said it lost its compression and it's all shelled out. He said he'd give me $50 to part it out."

"My son, my son," I said, "what are they teaching in graduate school nowadays? He's trying to rip you off. He says it's shelled out just so you'll take $50 for it. Always get a second opinion. Hang on to it until warm weather and I'll tow the Rabbit home to Lincoln where I know an honest mechanic. It's the least I can do for the best car I ever had. And listen, don't feel guilty."

"Golly, it's hard not to," he said. "It's only got 169,000 miles on it."

So when it got hot enough at the end of August, I rented one of those triangular towing bars ($17.64) and drove my '76 Dodge pickup to Iowa City. By the time I got back, I'd bought three tanks of gas ($72.93) and three pints of transmission fluid ($6.46) for the pickup. Hooking up the tow bar, I'd scraped my shins and grated my knuckles and got sweat in my eyes. But the Rabbit was back in Lincoln. I left it with my honest mechanic, said a few incantations, and waited.

Two days later he called with the bad news.

"Your Rabbit's dead," he said. "It lost its compression and it's shelled out. I'll give you $100 to part it out."

I went into voodoo deprivation shock.

"If the Rabbit gets no more miles to the gallon, what's that going to do to my pulse rate?" I asked my wife. "Will I even have a 61st birthday?"

"Don't be silly," she said. "Take the $100 and let him part it out. That's more than we'll get when we part you out." Then she laughed.

So we took the title to my mechanic and signed away the best car I ever owned.

"You said you'd give me $100," I reminded him.

"Oh, yeah," he said. "Let's see—you owe me $60 for the compression test, and $12 for the fuel filter we had to put on to see if it would start. That's $72 off the $100, so I owe you $28."

He wrote me a check and that night, I called my son.

"The Rabbit's dead," I said.

"Let me guess," he said. "It lost its compression and it's shelled out."

"Yes," I said. "But my honest mechanic gave me $100 to part it out. That's twice what you were going to get. Listen to your old dad and you'll save money."

"I wouldn't rush into it," he said. "Only $100 for the best car you ever owned? He's trying to rip you off. Why stop with a second opinion? There's that mechanic in Loveland you like. Why don't you tow it to Colorado?"

He's got a smart mouth. He got it from his mother.

"So let's see," she said, "you paid $73 for gas, $6 for transmission fluid, $17 for a tow bar. You towed it back to Lincoln where you got $22 less for it than if you'd left it in Iowa. And you scraped your shins and grated your knuckles and got sweat in your eyes. Why in the name of your penurious soul did you do all that?"

"To save money," I said. "Dammit, to save money."

So don't expect me to make fun of Republicans who want to cut taxes, increase defense spending, and thereby get out of debt. Like Dorothy and Toto and the Gipper, I know if you believe hard enough, what you want to happen just happens. It just does. And to hell with numbers.

Outta Gas

JANUARY 12, 1998

I don't normally like to go public with domestic discord, but I know my wife is going to blab this story to her friends. So hear my side first.

We're driving to Colorado, see, for the holidays, both to visit kids and grandkids and to spend time in the mountains. Whenever we're on the road, my wife and I have a running dispute: she likes to get gas when the tank is half full; I like to wait until there's maybe a half gallon left.

The high-water point of my driving career came in 1968 when we ran out of gas at 2 a.m. and managed to coast several hundred yards right up to the pumps of the only open gas station within 50 miles.

It was a masterpiece of fuel management, an automotive "Ode to Joy." We sat a moment in silence, save for the whimpering of the children.

"Well," my wife said, "we might as well get gas while we're here."

She was being sarcastic. She grew up in one of those families that keep their tanks full. Once when her mother was visiting, we ran out of gas in the Gateway parking lot.

"Isn't the gauge working?" my mother-in-law asked.

"Oh, grandma," my daughter wailed, "Daddy doesn't buy gas till we run out."

"After 20 years," my wife said, "you can get used to walking down a highway with a gas can."

God knows I've explained it often enough. It's physics. It's a question of inertia and drag. It goes like this:

A full tank weighs more than an empty tank. Weight increases inertia and drag. Increased inertia and drag play hell with your gas mileage. Ergo, the less gas in your tank, the more miles per gallon.

So people who drive around with full tanks, I instruct my family, might as well be throwing dollar bills out their car windows.

Now we're halfway between Ft. Morgan and Greeley and my wife is leaning over to look at the gas gauge.

"Shouldn't we get gas?" she asks. "Or would you rather freeze and starve halfway up the mountain?"

"Nolo problemo," I say. "The warning light isn't even on yet."

It comes on as I speak.

"There's a station right up there," she says.

"Wrong side of the road," I say. "Besides, we already know, don't we, that when the light comes on we have three gallons left. That'll take us 80 miles. We only have 60 to go. We'll get gas in the morning."

"What is it about feeling secure you don't like?" she asks.

"You wanna feel secure," I say, "you live in Sweden or some other socialist utopia. America's all about living close to the edge."

"You talk that way every time you get west of North Platte," she says. "Did you ever notice that?"

We get to the cabin all right, and next morning I'm ready to go the 11 miles into Estes for groceries. It's 15 degrees and the car won't start. I pop the hood. It's a '90 Toyota and what I see is nothing like what I see when I pop the hood of my '76 Dodge pickup. My wife comes out to watch.

"Electrical problem," I say. "But how's a man to fix an electrical problem when they hide the sparkplugs and distributor and magneto?"

"Maybe," she says, "it's run out of gas."

"Cars don't run out of gas when they're not running," I explain. "There was gas in it when we got here so there's gas in it now."

I wiggle some wires that might be sparkplug wires, knock against what could be a distributor, bang on three things which look nothing like a magneto, get back in the car and crank it. Nothing happens.

"Well," she says, shivering a little, "do you suppose we freeze first? Or starve to death?"

"No," I say. "We'll call the Toyota dealer in Ft. Collins and he'll fix it."

"It'll cost $294 to get it towed to Ft. Collins," she says. "But you'll get awfully good gas mileage on the way."

She's right. It will cost $294. So I call our neighbor. He comes over.

"Gas line freeze-up," I say.

"Outta gas," she says.

He takes me to town to get some de-icer. Says he needs to go in for gasoline anyway. Says he likes to keep the top half full.

"While we're there," he says, "we'll fill the gas can. Can't hurt."

When we get back, I put the de-icer in the tank and crank the engine. The battery sounds tired. The engine doesn't start.

"Try putting in the gas," my wife says.

"OK," I say, winking at my neighbor. "We'll humor the little woman."

It starts. She smiles. My neighbor looks away.

I have no idea what she'll make of this for her friends. But I think about it a while and I have a good idea of what I'll make of it:

By running out of gas, I just saved a $294 towing charge.

Can't wait to tell my kids. Might even give my mother-in-law a call.

Rapture

OCTOBER 10, 1994

At first, I was awfully disappointed to wake up a week ago Saturday to the realization that I'm not part of the Elect.

It was Oct. 1, and that meant The Rapture had come and gone, the saved had been whisked away to Heaven leaving only the unsaved behind, and even though I was wearing clean underwear in anticipation, I hadn't made the cut.

Don't act like you don't know what I'm talking about. You heard the news back in July the same as I did. That's when Harold Camping, via the 40 stations in his Family Radio Network, told us that judgment would come before Oct. 1.

He didn't just make it up either. He had numbers. The Rapture was set for sometime in September, 1994, just 2300 days after May of 1988, which was exactly 13,000 years after the creation of the universe in May of 11,013 B.C. (If that seems a little late, remember that in the beginning, God created fossils.)

Made sense to me.

I grew up in a church where we talked a lot about being the only ones in town who'd get raptured, so I've known since first grade that it was coming.

What surprises me, though, is how many have been left behind.

First thing I did when I saw that I was still here was to run out and buy a morning paper to see who was missing. I nearly got hit by a '89 Grand Marquis with a bumper sticker that read "In case of the Rapture, this car will be unoccupied." It had an occupant, and he was driving 15 mph over the speed limit.

There was nothing on the front page about anyone disappearing, so I turned to the sports page. That's where I was really shocked.

Bill McCartney and his Colorado football team were still around.

I was sure they were of the Elect after they beat Michigan 27-26 with a 64-yard touchdown on the last play of the game. It was a fundamentalist Protestant version of a Hail Mary pass—and a clear case of Divine Intervention.

"Those guys out there asked for a miracle," said a Colorado player on the sideline, "and God decided to give it to them."

Seemed highly irregular. Hadn't God used up His football eligibility back in Knute Rockne's day? Didn't Colorado have too many beings on the field? But the Michigan coach didn't take any of that to the NCAA. Probably remembered how the Red Sea closed around the enemies of the Chosen People.

So I figured surely Coach McCartney and his boys had been raptured. But the afternoon of Oct. 1, there they were on TV, generating spiritual energy from some source by holding hands on the sideline while they beat Texas 34-31 on a field goal with one second left.

Well, if McCartney hadn't made it, I thought, surely Jerry Falwell had. But there he was on TV too, still peddling his $43 videotapes of the Good News: President Clinton is implicated in the murder of "countless people."

I was certain Pat Robertson had heard the trumpet and been taken off in the twinkling of an eye. Pat often advises God on political matters, and thus knows all about Divine Intentions. Here's what he said about them last month:

"We are seeing the Christian Coalition rise to where God intends it to be in this nation—as one of the most powerful political forces that's ever been in the history of America."

So surely he wouldn't miss The Rapture.

But a story in *Newsweek* says Pat's still here, still selling his wide variety of Christian products including a face cream called "Sea of Galilee" and a nutritional drink called "The American Whey."

Ollie North's still around, too. So are Jesse Helms, Danny Quayle, Robert Dornan and lots of other politicians who regularly give us messages from God which have astonishingly convenient political implications.

I began thinking the unthinkable.

Can it be, I wondered, that it's false prophets who have taken over radio and TV and threaten to take over Congress? Can it be that ever' body talkin' 'bout Heaven ain't goin' there?

You might say in rebuttal that Harold Camping got mixed up on his dates, but since you're still here you would say that. But his numbers are hard to argue with, and so far as I know he hasn't been seen this month.

It's unsettling to be left behind, I admit, but incorrigible optimist that I am, I urge you to look at the bright side:

Since all of God's real spokesmen are playing harps by now, we don't have to listen to anyone who claims to be a source close to the Deity. That means we can get on with making the best of our depravity by reforming health care and campaign financing, and by passing all that other legislation that Jerry and Pat and Ollie say God is against.

I know that Nebraskans aren't much interested in those things this time of year, so let me tell you what else it means:

It means that on Oct. 29, we'll have a football game, not a religious dispute. Frazier won't be playing for Tom Osborne, but God won't be playing for Bill McCartney.

New Dog

MAY 7, 1990

Of course we don't set out to buy a defective dog.

Our previous pooch, Sherman, was the Patron Saint of Self-Effacing Mixed Breeds, but he developed lots of defects during his seventeenth and final year. So we are ready now for a dog with all his faculties gleaming, his teeth clean and sharp, his heart chugging away pocketa pocketa pocketa without a queep. In short, something in mint condition.

Instead, we get Ned, the One-Eyed Beagle.

He is the last one the breeder has left from the litter and it's easy to see why. The bad eye looks spooky—milky and set back deeper in his skull than his good one. But, the breeder tells us (and his vet confirms it over the telephone), it's probably not serious: a scratch on the retina that will heal in several days.

So we write a check and take our brand new pup home to admire his structural integrity.

Five days later, the eye doesn't look any better, maybe worse, so we take him to our old vet, the one who'd treated Sherman long after less wimpish owners would have put him to sleep, as we say in the dog game.

"Uh oh," he says when he sees the eye.

He tells us it is shot, irreparably damaged, forever no good. Ruptured, he says, and all the fluid drained out.

Ned is struggling to get away, crying and growling and trying to bite the vet's fingers. Aside from the eye, we ask, how does the vet like the pup?

Not much at all, it turns out. Ned has a terrible overbite and worst of all, even more serious than the bad eye, Ned is headstrong, he wants to dominate anyone he's around, and he's going to be hell to train. The vet can tell, he says, from the way Ned refuses to tolerate a hand atop his snout.

"You're not going to like him," he tells us. "You're going to be comparing him to Sherman and you're not going to like him."

The vet liked Sherman a lot because he never made a fuss when things were poked into his bodily orifices. He had both eyes, his jaws matched nicely, and he wasn't headstrong. He tolerated a hand atop his snout and he put up with being dominated.

He put up with nearly everything. That's why we had him canonized.

"I recommend you take the pup back to the breeder," the vet says. "Get a refund."

We wonder what we'll look like in the mirror if we send our defective dog back to the shop. He can't be fixed, and there's no market for headstrong, one-eyed Beagles with mismatched jaws, so we have a pretty good idea of what will happen to him: he'll be put to sleep, as we say in the dog game.

I tell my friend Mary Smith about the problem. She doesn't see it as a problem at all: a headstrong, one-eyed Beagle with mismatched jaws is a pearl of great price to be made over and crooned to and filled up with good things to eat. Because of, not despite, the defects. She buys me a stuffed dog to help me decide.

"Here's a dog without flaws," she says. "Boring, isn't it?

So we decide the hell with it, we'll keep the pup. You can't name a dog Ned and then take him back for a refund.

"We'll get a little eye-patch for him," my wife says.

"And a little pirate hat," my daughter says.

"And a little parrot to put on his shoulder," my son says.

"Yeah," I say. "We'll have fun."

And yet.

I look at that milky eye and I wonder how it would have been had we got to the breeder earlier in the day before the other puppies were sold. Then I worry that I'm such a tightwad I resent having bought damaged goods, and I wonder if Mary's joke is more than a joke.

I remember Hawthorne's scientist in "The Birthmark" who cannot tolerate the one flaw in his wife's beauty, who devises a treatment that erases the birthmark but kills the patient so that he ends up with an absolutely flawless corpse.

I lock my office door on Mary's stuffed dog and walk home through the snow, down the alley behind our house, through the back gate, past the frozen bed of day lilies where we buried Sherman.

"Whaddya think, Sherm?" I ask the snow.

Inside the warm house, Ned squints Popeye-like over the edge of his box, tumbles out, slithers and slides and bounces across the kitchen floor, making puppy yips all the way. He bumps into me because he's got no depth perception. He starts chewing on my pant leg, his upper and lower teeth not meeting right, and with his front end down and his rear end up, with tail all awag, he growls when I try to take my pant leg back. He seems glad to see me.

Travels with Ned

JANUARY 11, 1999

In the last—and most emphatic—of his seven rules of etiquette for attending funerals, Mark Twain tells us, "Do not bring your dog."

But ever since I read John Steinbeck's *Travels With Charley,* I've been hooked on the idea of taking my dog wherever I go.

Even to funerals.

Charley, you may remember, was Steinbeck's French Poodle—born and raised in a Paris suburb—who knew "a little poodle-English," but who responded "only to commands in French." His real name was Charles de Chien, and he and Steinbeck made an enviable pair traveling about the country in a pickup-camper named Rocinante after Don Quixote's horse.

I was so taken by the romance of it all that I forgot Twain's advice.

The trouble is that our dog isn't an elegant French Poodle named Charles le Chien. Our dog is a one-eyed Beagle with a headstrong personality and mismatched jaws. His name is Ned.

We don't take him to local funerals. But any time my wife and I travel to funerals so distant we have to be gone overnight, Ned goes too. Lest you think us odd, let me quickly add that he never goes into the church with us. He stays in the car and bays mournfully during the service. Sometimes in our pew we hear him. Sometimes those in other pews hear him. Sometimes even the guest of honor hears him.

I long ago gave up the notion that I was Steinbeck and Ned was Charles le Chien. But we continue taking Ned on overnight roadtrips because we don't know what else to do with him.

Our friends all know Ned so of course they won't keep him while we're gone. We've considered putting him up at one of those dog-boarding places, but Ned knows how to make himself an unwelcome guest. He bays.

On three occasions—when we got him fixed, when he jumped a '79 Buick coming down Adams Street, when he blew the anterior cruciate ligament in his right knee by cutting sharply to his left in pursuit of an agile squirrel—he's had to stay overnight at the vet's.

All three stays ended prematurely.

"You can come get him now," the vet would yell into the phone, trying to make himself heard over Ned's baying. "He recovered a lot faster than we thought he would."

So despite Twain's advice, we bring our dog. Travels with Ned are hardly anything like travels with Charley.

When we were bringing him home from the Beagle puppy farm, he gagged a couple of times, then barfed all over the front seat.

As he grew older, he quit barfing—but only on condition that we let him sit in the driver's lap. When he learned to operate the turn signals and the windshield wipers, we banished him to the back seat.

He insists we keep one of the back windows open a couple of inches so he can stick out the tip of his snout and get Beagle goober all over the outside of the glass for the amusement of other interstate travelers.

If we forget to open the window, he has ways of reminding us.

First he puts his snout to the top of the closed window and bays, getting Beagle goober all over the inside of the glass for the amusement of other interstate travelers.

If that doesn't work, he uses his Ultimate Weapon. He emits an offensive emission.

Ned's a talented Beagle. He can emit offensive emissions at will.

Beagle offensive emissions make mega-pig operations smell like a nosegay of lilacs. Beagle offensive emissions warp your sunglasses. Beagle offensive emissions inside a closed car make you consider bailing out at 75 mph.

So we surrender to Ned's olfactory terrorism. We open his window.

It's OK in nice weather, but when it's below zero, we get chilled.

I try to imagine what Steinbeck would have said to Charles le Chien. *"Plus de flatulence terrible! N'est-ce pas?"*

I tell Ned that on our next trip we'll take our '76 highway-orange Dodge pickup and he'll have to ride in the back.

I show him an *LJS* clipping from last summer about a German shepherd named Copper who was forced to ride in the back of his owner's pickup (no reason given, but I'm thinking offensive emissions), and was sucked out by a ferocious crosswind on Highway 2 near Nebraska City.

"Any more *flatulence terrible*," I tell Ned, "and you'll be riding in the back of the pickup and get sucked out by a ferocious crosswind."

But he knows an empty threat when he hears one. He knows we'd never be so gauche as to drive to a funeral in a '76 highway-orange Dodge pickup.

Even one with that certain *je ne sais quoi* air that comes with a one-eyed Beagle goobering up the windows and emitting offensive emissions.

New People in Town

MARCH 29, 1993

"It's kind of scary," a Lexington resident says about the ethnic diversity attracted by the meat packing plant out there. "There's a lot of new people in town."

That must be the way Dolores Sanchez felt when Jimmie Lee Johnson and I blew into Clayton, N.M., in the summer of 1954. She lived there and we were new people in town. She was Hispanic and we were Anglo. She was cashier at the Hacienda Cafe and we wanted to eat without having the money to pay for it. Here's how it was:

I'm 20 years old and about to go into the army. The little town in southwest Kansas where I've been trying to grow up is too respectable for a proper sendoff, so Jimmie Lee and I drive 260 miles west to Raton, N.M., for a weekend of wickedness. We're going to drink beer and bet horses.

There's more ethnic diversity there than we're used to—funny names on everything, including the race track, La Mesa Park, where a lot of people in the stands aren't speaking English. So we feel pretty smug when we win nearly $100 on Friday, but we lose most of it back on Saturday, and that night we drink our last warm beer in our scuzzy $4-a-night motel and plot our way through Sunday's Racing Form. It doesn't work: going into the last race of the day, we haven't cashed a ticket.

We have $2.53 between us, just enough gas money to get home.

But in the ninth race we see a horse—Manifest Destiny II—whose odds are way too long. He's 4–1 to win and he was closing fast last time he ran a mile and half. We're pretty sure we've handicapped this one more carefully than the others in the stands, and we know that's when you should bet. Even if you have only $2.53 and you're 260 miles from home with less than half a tank of gas and you haven't eaten since breakfast.

So we buy a $2 win ticket on Manifest Destiny II. He runs a good race but comes in a half-length behind a raggedy 22-1 longshot named Speedy Gonzalez that shouldn't have been on the track in the first place.

So there's nothing to do but start driving east. We figure we'll go until we get to the last town we can get to without running out of gas, then see what happens.

It turns out to be Clayton, 105 miles down Highway 64. It's 9 p.m. and it's been ten hours since our eggs and hashbrowns, so we slide into a booth in the Hacienda Cafe, order four hamburgers with fries, and two chocolate malts.

We consider just running out without paying. But we'd have to go by the beefy guy eating the banana cream pie at the counter—the sheriff for all we know. And our car's parked under a streetlight bright enough that you can read the license plate from inside the cafe.

So we decide to rely on the kindness of strangers. I had a speech class in college, so I start.

"I'm going in the army next week," I tell the girl behind the register. "We're about out of gas and we don't have enough money to pay for this and I'm going in the army next week."

She's about our age, maybe a year or two older, black haired and dark eyed, pretty, I think, in an ethnically diverse way. She looks at us and doesn't say anything. I wonder if she speaks English.

"We had $2.53," Jimmie Lee explains, "but we bet $2 on the last race at Raton."

"Let me guess how your horse ran," she says, like she's talking to two kids.

"He lost," I say. "And I'm going in the army next week."

"I bet you are," she says, "but what are you going to do now?"

She looks at our $2.60 bill. The beefy guy has finished his banana cream pie and is looking at us over his coffee.

"I'd write a check," I say, "but I don't have one. If you got one for your bank, I could cross out the name and write in my bank. It works. I've done it before."

"Not here you haven't," she says. "We don't take out-of-town checks."

I don't say anything. Jimmie Lee snorts the kind of laugh guys in my hometown snort when they don't know what else to do. The beefy guy is grinning now, but it's not a friendly grin.

"Well, shoot," I say. "I don't know."

"I suppose I could make you a loan," she says. "Is that what you're asking?"

I try to think of what John Wayne might say, but I can't.

“Well, yeah,” I say. “Okay.”

“It’d be real nice,” Jimmie Lee says. “We’d appreciate it.”

So she pulls a coin purse from under the counter and takes out three wrinkled ones, four quarters, and two halves.

“Take five,” she says. “You need gas. Standard’s supposed to stay open till ten, but sometimes they close early. You better hurry.”

We take her $5, pay the bill, and get her lovely name—Dolores Sanchez—so we can send her the money tomorrow. Then we back out the cafe door, grinning and thanking her and saying if she’s ever in trouble in our town she should look us up.

We drive in silence down Highway 64, digesting it all.

“I’ll be damned,” Jimmie Lee finally says.

“Me too,” I say.

Compost Pile

MAY 20, 1991

It comes on me again while I'm down on my knees, my head bowed, digging out a hole for another tomato plant and taking almost too much pleasure in the velvety feel of the dirt I'm fondling. I'm worshipping, I find myself thinking, at the altar of my compost pile. That means I've fallen into my Walt Whitman syndrome again.

"Behold this compost!" I exult in a frenzy of direct quotation, "behold it well!"

A squirrel running along the top of the garden fence stops and looks interested, so it's time for me to go inside. I meet my wife in the kitchen, my fingers rich with garden, sweat dripping off my nose.

"I make holy whatever I touch or am touched from," I inform her, "the scent of these armpits aroma finer than prayer!"

"Good grief," she says, "you've fallen into your Walt Whitman syndrome again, haven't you? You've been playing in that compost too long."

I think she means too long on this particular day, but maybe she means too long in more cosmic terms. I've been composting my garden for 21 years now and I've grown extravagantly fond of my dirt. When I fall into my Walt Whitman syndrome, I imagine that the dirt returns my affection, that there's a current of spiritual electricity between the two of us. It grows out of the annual routine I religiously follow:

In November after the leaves have fallen, I put them inside my snow-fence compost enclosure and water them down. During the next twelve months I add potato peels, grass clippings, carrot scrapings, dog droppings, the leftover broccoli we forgot about in the back of the refrigerator until it was covered with mold—any manner of nastiness at all so long as it's organic. Then in the following November, I rototill the year-old compost into the garden. By spring it has magically disappeared and the dirt has become moist and rich-smelling and, as we say in the composting game, friable as all get out. It whimpers for seed.

That's when Walt Whitman starts making sense to me. That's when I sound my own barbaric yawps as I dig in my glorious May dirt.

Sure, I know: by the end of August, a sterner reality will set in. That same dirt will be compacted to the hardness of concrete, weeds will be everywhere, cucumber plants will drop dead overnight just as they're about to earn their keep, the bottoms of the Big Boys will go rotten and melt into the ground they rest on because once again they'll have escaped their tomato cages. And I'll be up to my aromatic armpits in zucchini.

But none of that matters. The real payoff in my garden isn't the beans and tomatoes and peppers that fill my stomach; it's the nectar and ambrosia that intoxicate my soul.

I've been influenced in all this by my Uncle Roy in California who took his Kansas need to grow vegetables with him when he went west. He composts everything he can get his hands on, spreads it on his garden, and improves the diets of the lotus-eaters out there by force-feeding them his good homegrown vegetables.

"Poison-free okra! Hey!" he shouts at them, implying that Safeway's okra is hellbent on shriveling them up like a DDTed mosquito. "No herbicides on this eggplant! Listen!" he yells, as though Piggly Wiggly's eggplant is daily doused with Agent Orange.

So I've inherited a gene that predisposes me to believe that if compost won't fix it, it doesn't need fixed. That means the bugs eat as many of our beans as we do, that what we call our lawn is mostly dandelions and Creeping Charlie, with here and there a clump of Kentucky bluegrass wondering what it's doing in such company.

But really committed composters say that doesn't matter either. We walk around whistling in close harmony with what we're pleased to imagine is the music of the spheres. The goofiest of us may even see the earth as Walt Whitman did, a vast and lovely compost pile that brings beauty out of ugliness, life out of death. I look at the day lilies conspiring to bloom as they rise out of the backyard grave of our previous dog, St. Sherman, and I understand Walt's sense that something magic is happening.

"What chemistry!" he shouts, sounding a little like Uncle Roy, that "grows such sweet things out of such corruptions," that "distills such exquisite winds out of such infused fetor," that "gives such divine materials to men, and accepts such leavings from them at last."

That may be a funny way to talk about grass clippings and dog droppings and moldy broccoli, but old Walt knew that when you worship at the altar of a compost pile on a sunny May morning, you take your Transcendence where you find it.

School Prayer

JANUARY 29, 1996

Some of my colleagues in the American Association of Dirty Rotten Secular Humanists got upset recently when Rep. Ernest Istook (R-OK) introduced a constitutional amendment to allow student-sponsored prayer in public schools.

The concern was that as an alleged conservative, Rep. Istook wasn't showing proper respect for the wishes of the Founding Fathers, especially as they're expressed in the First Amendment's dirty rotten secular humanist Establishment Clause: "Congress shall make no law respecting an establishment of religion."

But you don't hear me squawking.

That's because I have no objection to anybody praying to the divinity of their choice in public schools or anywhere else. I say if it feels good, do it.

All I ask is that they do it right: if they profess to be Christian they should follow biblical instructions. When it comes to prayer in the schools, I'm a fundamentalist. I believe in the inerrancy of those scriptures I agree with. Especially the red-letter part where Jesus is quoted directly.

And you know what Jesus says about praying, don't you? Of course you do. But let me remind you.

In the Sermon on the Mount, Jesus says this to the disciples:

"And when thou prayest, thou shalt not be as the hypocrites are: for they love to pray standing in the synagogues and in the corners of the streets, that they may be seen of men. Verily I say unto you, They have their reward.

"But thou, when thou prayest, enter into thy closet, and when thou hast shut thy door, pray to thy Father which is in secret; and thy Father which seeth in secret shall reward thee openly."

So if that's the kind of praying Rep. Istook means—and surely it is since he's a Christian—why should we get upset over prayer in the schools?

Imagine the scene. Third grade arithmetic class. Test in progress. Johnny raises his hand.

"Please, ma'am," he says. "I need divine guidance on question #3 and the Istook Amendment guarantees me the right to ask for it."

"So it does," Miz Smith says, just before she lapses into King James English, "but you have to enter into thy closet to get it. Be thou careful of the brooms and mops. And be thou sure to shut the door lest ye be seen and heard of men, and thought a hypocrite. Remember, Jesus liketh not little showoffs."

So Johnny runs off to find the janitor to unlock the closet for him. He comes back a few minutes later, a beatific smile on his face and the answer to question #3 in his head.

Now who could object to such a scene? Certainly not me.

And that must be the kind of praying Rep. Istook has in mind—prayer that would be a confidential communication that only sender and receiver are privy to, with no hint of hypocrisy or ulterior motive, no whiff of holier-than-thou perfume, and certainly no suggestion of any intimidation of those fellow students who know the answer to question #3 without resorting to divine guidance.

In short, the kind of prayer that might be offered up in a closed closet.

Some of you might argue that I interpret "closet" too literally here, that Jesus didn't really mean we should get in there with the brooms and mops when we pray, that "closet" is just a metaphor for privacy.

If you want to start down that slippery slope of seeing metaphor in Holy Writ, I guess that's your business. But don't ask me to help.

Besides, if the closet is simply a metaphor for privacy, what could be more private than praying silently without telling anyone else what you're doing? And if that's what Jesus meant, why would we need a constitutional amendment to allow it in schools? Silent prayers would fall into the don't ask-don't tell category—like dirty thoughts and other interior monologues—and all of that's already allowable. How could it not be?

Which gets at what super-suspicious dirty rotten secular humanists are worried about. What if Rep. Istook has something else in mind besides silent prayer or closet prayer? What if he means the kind of audible, external, non-spontaneous, organized prayer meetings that pressure the little children to either join in or stay awake all night worrying about going to hell?

If that's what the amendment means, then we all ought to worry. It already has 101 co-sponsors. If it gets two-thirds approval in the House and Senate, then is ratified by 38 states in the next seven years, we'd be turning our children and grandchildren into scriptural scofflaws. As a school prayer fundamentalist, I'm afraid we'd be held responsible.

Remember what Jesus said about the street-corner prayer mongers (and if the closet is a metaphor, maybe the street corner is too): "Verily I say unto you, They have their reward."

I don't know about you, but that scares hell out of me.

Static Cling

FEBRUARY 24, 1997

I always thought those ads about the Heartbreak of Static Cling were overblown. Maybe it's because in our household division of labor, I do the things I like to do—cook and drive my pickup to the dump—and my wife does the rest, including the laundry. So maybe I'm not sufficiently sensitive about static cling.

At least not until about a month ago.

I know it was about a month ago because it always takes me about a month before I can talk about things like this.

The story begins when I have a nightmare in early January. I dream that I haven't made the 1997 Stud-Muffins of the English Department calendar. There are only seven males in our English Department, and in my dream the other six get two months each and I don't get any. The dream ends when a student asks me why my picture isn't there and I lose all professorial dignity. I say "I don't even know what a stud-muffin is," then I laugh wildly—like an Edgar Allen Poe character—and hot tea comes out my nose.

It's just a dream.

But still it pushes me to two January resolutions: I resolve to maintain professorial dignity throughout 1997, and I further resolve to transform my body. I'll get Really Muscular and then we'll see whose picture gets in the 1998 Stud-Muffins of the English Department calendar.

If there should happen to be one.

So here I am in the men's locker room of the field house. I've just worked up a sweat trotting a few times around the indoor track, and I've made a few little grunty noises on the weight machines. A couple of coeds had noticed me and have whispered to each other while smiling at me.

So I can feel myself on the verge of becoming Really Muscular and calendar-worthy as I come out of the shower dripping wet and buck naked. I'm not sure how buck naked is different than plain naked, but I like the macho sound of it.

And I feel a macho kinship with a couple of burly students who are getting dressed while they talk about abs and pecs and lats. I'm not sure what abs and pecs and lats are, but I look forward to getting some and joining the discussion in a couple of weeks.

Tightening my stomach so it won't sag, I grab my freshly laundered and folded towel, authoritatively snap it out of its fold, and watch something that has been statically clinging to it go flying across the locker room.

It's a pair of my wife's lace-trimmed unmentionables.

My first impulse is to pretend I didn't see them fly across the locker room. I consider just walking by them on the way out and with great professorial dignity saying something like "I believe there's a pair of lace-trimmed unmentionables lying here on the floor of the men's locker room. Wherever might they have come from?"

But then I remember that my wife said she paid $2.49 for them in the Unmentionables Department at Target, so I walk across the room and pick them up. I'd like to jam them in my pocket, but I'm still buck naked so I walk back to my locker and stuff them inside my bag.

When I look up, the two burly guys look down. They've stopped talking about abs and pecs and lats. They've stopped talking about everything. Their ears are red. One of them makes a little snorting noise, like a startled horse.

I think they've seen my wife's lace-trimmed unmentionables. But I don't think they know they're hers.

I want to say something like "That's right, Bucko. I wear lace-trimmed unmentionables." Or "Do you prefer the full cut or the French cut? Double layered crotch or single?" Or "So's your old man."

You know, something wonderfully suave and debonair.

But it's hard to be wonderfully suave and debonair when you're buck naked and 63 years old. So I don't say anything.

I dry off and quickly attire myself in professorial dignity: boxers, tee shirt, pants, socks, shoes, shirt, tweed sports jacket with leather elbow patches. Only then do I look again at the two weight lifters. They're still looking at the floor and they're still not saying anything. They're catatonic.

As I leave, one of them is finally able to look me in the eye. I see the flicker of a smile. It doesn't look the way I imagine a smile of macho kinship might look.

"M'love," I say to my wife when I get home that evening, "could you maybe use some of that static cling stuff on your lace-trimmed unmentionables?"

She gives me a look and pours us both some tea.

"Let me guess," she says after a minute or two. "This has something to do with the Stud-Muffins of the English Department calendar you're always mumbling about at 2 a.m."

"Don't be silly," I say. "I don't even know what a stud-muffin is."

Then I laugh wildly—like an Edgar Allen Poe character—and hot tea comes out my nose.

Straight Choice

FEBRUARY 15, 1993

"Tell me one more time," she says, putting down the front section of the Sunday paper. "Why was it right for Truman to integrate African-Americans into the military and wrong for Clinton to integrate homosexuals?"

Her brow is furrowed and the tip of her tongue is sticking out the corner of her mouth. She's cute when she tries to understand male logic.

"Well, my dear," I say over the top of the sports section, "it's really awfully simple if you look at it non-judgmentally. It's wrong to segregate on the basis of race because race isn't something we choose. But homosexuals do choose their disgustingly wicked sexual orientation. If they don't like the consequences, they can just by golly choose to be straight."

"My goodness," she says. "That is awfully simple, isn't it?"

She turns to the editorial page and I go back to the sports section, happy to have explained it so well. A minute or two later she looks up again.

"When did you choose?" she asks.

"When did I choose what?" I say. I'm trying to focus on yet another story about how Jimmy Johnson brought the Cowboys from a 1-15 season to the Super Bowl win.

"When did you choose your heterosexual orientation?" she says.

"It's not about choosing to be heterosexual," I say, not unkindly. "It's about choosing to be homosexual."

"But," she says, "if we say homosexuals made the wrong choice in choosing to be gay, doesn't that mean the rest of us made the right choice in choosing to be straight? So when did you choose?"

I'm amused by her naivete, but I don't want to hurt her feelings so I blow my nose to disguise my snort.

"You don't understand, my love," I say. "We don't have to choose to be straight. We just are. It's like we don't have to choose to breathe oxygen. We just do. We can't help it."

"It's funny," she says. "I can't remember when I chose to be straight either. You'd think we could remember something that important. You remember how wetting your pants in first grade made you choose not to be a Republican. I remember how grading high school English essays made me choose to be an elementary librarian. But neither one of us can remember when we chose to be straight instead of gay. Doesn't that strike you as funny?"

"You're not listening," I say gently. Then I speak very slowly and enunciate very carefully, like George Bush saying no new taxes. "Straights don't have to choose to be straight. We're born that way. Gays choose to be not straight. Gays choose to be gay. So they have to live with the consequences. Now let's read the paper."

She's quiet for another minute or two.

"Doesn't quite seem fair, does it?" she says. "Why do they get to choose and we don't?"

"He's a helluva coach, isn't he?" I say. "Ol' Jimmy Johnson."

"You know what else is funny?" she says.

"No," I say. "What else is funny?"

"It's funny homosexuals would choose an orientation that gets them bashed, ridiculed, and condemned to hellfire for being abominations against God. Why would anyone choose that?"

"Got me," I say. Sometimes if I play dumb, she drops the subject.

"You know what I think?" she says. "I think we can't remember when we chose to be straight because not being straight was never an option. If being straight is our only option, then maybe being gay is their only option."

"Maybe so," I say, turning to the comics page.

"You know what else I think?" she says. "If they don't have an option, it doesn't seem right to discriminate against them."

"Um," I say, bringing my massive analytical powers to bear on "Mary Worth."

"So that brings me back to the original question," she says. "Why was it right for Truman to integrate African-Americans and wrong for Clinton to integrate gays?"

"You weren't paying attention to anything I said, were you?" I say, putting down the comics and talking loud. Sometimes you have to talk loud to get the message through. "IT'S BECAUSE WE DON'T CHOOSE OUR RACE BUT GAYS DO CHOOSE THIER SEXUAL ORIENTATION. IF THEY DON'T WANT TO BE DISCRIMINATED AGAINST, LET THEM CHOOSE TO BE STRAIGHT."

"Saying it louder doesn't convince anyone," she says. "Saying it louder means your logic has just blown a fuse. But I'll ask one more time: If gays choose to be gay instead of straight, when did you choose to be straight instead of gay?"

My legs cross involuntarily. I take a deep breath.

"I don't know," I say as quietly as I can. "It was a long, long time ago."

"About the time, I'll bet," she says, "that you decided to be Caucasian instead of African-American."

I give up then. You can't teach a woman to think like a man.

Dental Floss Incident

SEPTEMBER 22, 1997

I see bankruptcy ahead. I see a man once nestled in a comfy life of shabby gentility, his aristocratic mustache and goatee twisted by despair and poverty, hurling himself from a window, his elbow-patched mustard-and-green sports coat flapping madly in the wind. It's me.

I don't want to wallow in self-pity, but I'm the only member of our family who properly values frugality.

I was reminded anew of that fact last week when my son called to say that he and a friend were pitting their fathers against each other in a tightwad contest and I was way ahead. He seemed more amused than proud, as though the game had all the dignity of, say, a flatulence competition.

It had started, he said, when he told his friend that I used to embarrass my family by pulling our 1966 GMC Handivan up to the truck pumps where the gasoline was two cents a gallon cheaper.

"We can't get gas from truck pumps," my wife would tell me. "This is a passenger vehicle."

"This is a GMC," I'd say yet one more time. "There is no car called a GMC. Only trucks are called GMCs. Ergo, this is a truck and no matter how many passengers it carries, it's entitled to cheap gas from truck pumps."

"We're about to get arrested," my daughter would explain to her brother.

Personally, I don't see that as a story about tightwaddedness. It's about the American Way. Buy low, sell high. Two pennies saved are two pennies earned.

So my son's friend told about his father going to a fund-raiser concert where he was asked for a donation at the door. He refused, arguing that a donation is by definition money freely given, not money exchanged for goods or services. They didn't let him in. But it's something to think about.

My son came back with the story of my new Rockport shoes that make me walk funny because they're too small. They didn't have my size on the sale table—$90 shoes for $35—but who could pass up a bargain like that? When my kids snickered, I said I walked funny all the way to the bank to deposit the $55 I saved.

They traded more stories: his father doesn't eat at any restaurant without two-for-one coupons; I once got the family a free meal by crashing an employee party in a new Denny's that wouldn't be open to the public until next day.

Then he scored big: his father saved old bubble gum on the grounds that after a week it regained its flavor. I personally don't believe in the resurrection of bubble gum flavor. But still it's something to think about.

My son's retaliation was massive: he remembered the Dental Floss Incident.

It starts when my dental hygienist scolds me for not flossing.

"The floss gets stuck in my teeth," I tell her. "It looks like spinach."

"Get better floss," she says. "Cheap floss sticks in your teeth. Try this."

She gives me some space-age teflon-coated floss. It works so well that after it's gone I go looking for more.

And I find out what it costs: $3.99 for 54.7 yards. The house brand I usually buy is only $2.99 for 200 yards. Lots of people see those prices and think the good stuff is only a dollar more than the cheap stuff. They don't do the math.

I do the math. The house brand is 1.5 cents a yard; the good stuff is 7.2 cents a yard. Nearly five times as much.

My first impulse is to buy the house brand, but I remember it looks like spinach stuck in my teeth. I buy the good stuff and think of ways to recoup.

I could floss only once every five days and break even. But my dental hygienist intimidates me.

I could use two-inch lengths instead of ten-inch lengths. But I can't wrap two-inch lengths around my fingers to get the required leverage.

Then I hit on the solution: I could use each piece of floss five times instead of one time. We don't throw away our toothbrushes after one use, do we?

And the teflon coating makes the new stuff nearly indestructible. I could probably use it 10 times, 20 times, but I just want to stay even, not get ahead.

So I keep my used floss under my electric shaver in the vanity drawer where my wife won't find it—at least, not until we have a birthday party for our grandson and she's looking for a match to light the candles. She makes what for her is a horrifying discovery.

"Why," she asks, dangling the evidence in front of kids, grandkids, and in-laws, "is there used dental floss under your electric shaver in the vanity drawer?"

"Hah?" I say.

"You save old dental floss?" my daughter-in-law politely asks.

"He re-uses it!" my daughter shouts. "The poor old booger re-uses his dental floss!"

"Great move!" my son says, bursting into applause.

"Someday you'll all understand," I say, looking around for an open window to hurl myself from. "Someday all this will be yours."

Ebonics

JANUARY 27, 1997

I've been harboring a commoner's grudge against Prince Charles for the last couple of years, ever since the AP caught him looking down his aristocratic Windsor nose at American English.

Real English, he sniffed, "to my way of thinking means English English," and Americans have had a "very corrupting" influence on it because we "tend to invent all sorts of nouns and verbs and make words that shouldn't be."

He sounded downright French.

And you know what I said? I said "Well, la-de-damn-da." It's a phrase I learned in Meade County, Kansas, while I was acquiring the local version of corrupt English in my misspent youth.

I used to feel guilty about contributing to language corruption with that kind of talk. I knew Prince Charles would never say "La-de-damn-da" and many nights I sobbed myself to sleep on my wet pillow.

Then I read some descriptive linguistics and I wept no more.

Descriptive linguists are interested in describing how the language actually works—as opposed to prescriptive linguists who are interested in prescribing how it ought to work.

Descriptive linguistics relieved my stress about the way the English language—including mine—was going all to hell in a handbasket. Prince Charles might feel better if he'd read some too.

He'd find out, for example, that somebody has always been corrupting the English language. Before Americans and Australians, it was the Norse marauders and the Norman French (who conquered most of England in 1066 and thereafter considered English a minor French dialect).

He'd find out that without such corruptions, he'd still be saying the Lord's Prayer in the English of 1,000 years ago: "Faeder ure, thu the eart on heofonum, si thin nama gehalgod." And how would God like it if we talked that way about Him? He'd probably lay a plague of umlauts on us.

And it occurs to me that all those people having hissy fits about Ebonics—that African-American talk that's always inventing nouns and verbs and making words that shouldn't be—might also find some relief if they'd just take a deep breath, breathe out slowly through puffed cheeks, and settle down with a hot cup of cocoa and a book of descriptive linguistics.

They'd find that not only is English always in a state of flux, it's also made up at any given time of the dialects of a whole lot of speech communities based on geography, social class, age, profession, and so forth. That's why nobody but a lawyer can understand Lawyerese.

And here's the kicker: descriptive linguists would tell them that the dialects of those speech communities aren't better or worse, more moral or immoral, smarter or dumber. Just different.

They'd tell them that what we call Standard English didn't come down from Mt. Sinai on stone tablets; it's just another dialect. But it had the good luck to be the dialect of the most influential and moneyed and prestigious speakers in 14th and 15th century London. And—surprise!—they decided it was standard and all the others—Cockney, Yorkshire, Brooklyn, Louisiana, Ebonics—were sub-standard.

And being easily cowed by our social betters, we commoners bought it.

So most of us think that speakers of all those non-standard dialects are trying to sound like Bonnie Prince Charlie and not making it. But descriptive linguists tell us that all languages and all dialects have their own internal rules, that Ebonics is as rule-bound as Standard English. They're just different rules.

Les Whipp has already explained how acknowledging Ebonics in the Oakland schools can be a way of leading students to Standard English (*LJS*, Jan. 23), and that would be good practical education. Standard English is still where the money and the power and the prestige are, and anyone who wants a share of that had better be fluent in the money-power-prestige dialect, not because it's inherently better than other dialects, but because you need it to get on.

But, some of you are saying, surely I don't mean that all dialects are linguistically equal.

Of course I don't. All dialects are equal but one, and it's more noble, pure, high-minded, sweetly sonorous, elegant and subtle than all the others. It's the one spoken in Meade County, Kansas. Well, maybe not now. A lot of newcomers have moved in. And probably not in the whole county. Just the dialect north of the tracks in my hometown between, say, 1934 and 1952.

That's where we knew enough to say "oyce" instead of "always," where double negatives signaled we were serious ("I don't want no more fried liver") and triple negatives signaled we were really serious ("I don't never want no more fried liver").

And it's where the proper response to royal assertions that one small speech community had cornered the good English market was "Well, la-de-damn-da."

Resolution

JANUARY 15, 1996

"Here we are halfway through January," I tell my wife, "and I still haven't come up with a New Year's resolution to improve myself."

She looks up from the newspaper and rolls her eyes.

"Maybe there's no improvement possible," she says. "Maybe you've achieved perfection."

You'd have to hear her say it to know she's being sarcastic.

"OK, Miss Smartypants," I say, "what can you think of to make me a better person in 1996?"

"Here," she says, handing me a two-week-old editorial cartoon. "Does this give you any ideas?"

It's one of those New Year's cartoons showing 1996 as a little kid in diapers and 1995 as an old guy with a cane and white beard. The kid is saying "Anything I'm going to need to help me handle the presidential campaign?" The old guy is saying "A pooper-scooper."

"Do you mean," I say, wearing that steely-eyed, seriously constipated look future leaders always wear when they first catch a glimpse of their destiny, "that I should resolve to run for President in '96?"

She sees something very funny in the obituaries and laughs out loud. I know she's not laughing at my presidential aspirations because I have political experience. Didn't I, in 1972, come within a few thousand votes of being elected to the Lower South Platte Natural Resources District Board?

"I mean," she says, "that you should resolve to use your natural talent. You should resolve to be the pooper-scooper for the dog."

It's something she's been after me to do for several years now, ever since that warm spring day when Ned, our one-eyed Beagle with the headstrong personality and the mismatched jaws, dropped a load on someone else's yard.

"Thanks a lot, buddy!" a disembodied voice from behind the screen door told me. "I'll bring my dog over to crap in your yard sometime."

His attitude, I must say, came as a shock to me. I'd noticed that where Ned dropped his loads in our yard, luxuriant clumps of neon-green grass made the rest of the lawn look malnourished. So I'd always thought Ned was doing people a favor by organically fertilizing their lawns. I thought of him as a canine Johnny Appleseed going about improving the environment.

But when the disembodied voice behind the screen door offered to have his dog return the favor in our yard, I had a minor epiphany.

"Hey," I said to my wife. "I don't think I'd like to have somone else's dog drop a load in our yard."

"Then," said she, getting right to the heart of the matter, "you shouldn't let our dog drop a load in someone else's yard."

So I try. Before every walk, I look Ned in his one good eye and I say "Remember now, no load-dropping in other people's yards. How'd you like it if the St. Bernard down the street dropped his load in your yard?"

In the interest of scientific inquiry, Ned says, he wouldn't mind at all. That way we could compare the resulting clumps of grass to see which was neon-greener. He's pretty sure he'd win.

And, always litigious, Ned wants to negotiate: He won't drop his load in someone else's yard if he can drop it in the space between the sidewalk and the street.

He's got a point. I know from my '72 NRD campaign that you can't plant political signs there because it's in the street right-of-way. So technically, it's not part of someone's yard.

My wife demurs.

"If you can't put political crap there," she says—an insensitive reference to my NRD signs—"then you can't put dog crap there either."

She clinches her argument when she shows me a clipping about a guy in Oregon who videotaped someone else's Lhasa Apso dropping a load on his lawn. He made copies for the police and was in the process of charging the Lhasa Apso's owner with "offensive littering and criminal mischief"—punishable by a $1,000 fine. I gulp.

"Better get used to it," she says. "If yahoos like you don't clean up after their dogs, Lincoln's going to have a law like that and you'll get sent so far up the river we'll have to pipe soup to you."

So now when we take Ned for walks, we carry baggies and a brown paper sack. When he drops a load, we put a baggie over our hand like a surgical glove without fingers, pick up the load, turn the baggie inside out and put the whole thing in the brown sack without ever making direct contact with the bad stuff.

That's what my wife does anyway. I tried once, but it was all steamy and squishy and awful and I didn't like handling it at all.

She says I need more fire in my gut. She says if I don't get over my squeamishness, I'll never be able to run for President. And even if I got elected, she says, how could I ever handle Congress?

Sixty

JANUARY 17, 1994

Let me say right now that, no matter what my wife says, my 60th birthday this week is no big deal.

She says "Don't think of it as your 60th birthday; think of it as the first day of your seventh decade."

She says "Timothy Leary claims he gets high on senility; you'll have lots of fun."

She says "You poor old booger, you."

When she talks to the grandbabies on the phone, she asks them how many teeth they have now, then tells them that grandpa's teeth are going bad because he's nearly sixty, the poor old booger.

"Can you say 'poor old booger'?" she asks them. It knocks her out.

I know what she's up to. She's trying to jolly me out of what she thinks is the trauma of my 60th birthday.

"I'm not traumatized," I keep telling her. "It's just another birthday. The number happens to end in zero. It's no big deal."

"Funny you should say that," she says, "because when you turned 30 you wrote a pastoral elegy called 'Farewell my Youth, Alas, O!' When you turned 40, you went into midlife crisis by buying two old rustbucket Mercedes that didn't run, and when you turned 50 you stayed in bed all day with a pillow over your head."

She exaggerates. I didn't buy the second Mercedes until six weeks after I turned 40. The pillow wasn't over my head the whole day.

And let me also say right now that backing through the garage door last week to get to my dentist had nothing to do with my 60th birthday.

It wasn't my fault. First, I couldn't find the little appointment card to see what time I was supposed to be there, then I couldn't find my glasses to read it, then I couldn't find the car keys to get there on time.

And it certainly wasn't my fault the electric garage door opener didn't work right. It raised the door three feet, then stopped. It's not my electric garage door anyway. It's my wife's. I've never liked it.

She tells me I should always look in the rearview mirror when I back out of the garage. Even when I use our electric garage door opener.

"It's your electric garage door opener," I say. "I don't trust electric garage doors."

She also tells me I should never take the little gizmo that makes the electric garage door open and put it on top of the car. If I do that, she says, I might drive off with it still up there.

That's hard to remember when you're clearing away pieces of splintered garage door and broken taillights and the little whatchamacallit that squirts water on the car's back window. Besides, I'm in a big hurry to pay the dentist a lot of money to put another gold crown on my bad teeth. Gold crowns cost even more than electric garage door openers. That's what I'm thinking about when I drive off with the gizmo that opens the garage door—or used to before I backed through it—still on top of the car.

None of this has anything to do with my 60th birthday.

About three blocks later I hear a clattering sound on the car roof and I look in the rearview mirror—where my wife tells me I should have looked before I backed through the electric garage door—and I see something bouncing down the middle of 56th Street.

Five blocks further and it occurs to me that it might have been the gizmo my wife tells me never to put on the top of the car, so I turn around to pick it up. But by the time I get there, a guy is just getting back in his car with something in his hand.

"That's my gizmo!" I yell as he drives off in the direction of my dentist. By the time I get the car turned around, he's disappeared.

They're nice to me at the dentist's office when I explain why I'm late. They smile and whisper something to one another, but I'm pretty sure they aren't whispering that my 60th birthday is coming up. Still, they do have my date of birth in their files.

When I finally get home, I get tangled in the seat belt trying to get out of the car and throw my back out again. My wife watches out the window.

"What happened to the garage door?" she asks. "Where's the gizmo?"

"I'm still 59 years old," I say, trying to straighten up, "and I don't want to talk about it."

"There, there," she says. "We'll get you a new electric garage door for your birthday next week. And we'll go out to this nice restaurant where they cut up meat for old-timers. After that, we can go see 'Grumpy Old Men.' We'll have fun. You poor old booger, you."

I give up then.

"Just put me in the sun in my deck chair," I say, "and don't forget my laprobe."

Semi-Apology

FEBRUARY 12, 1996

An open letter to the white-haired gentleman on whose windshield I kicked snow while he was stopped at 48th and St. Paul at 4:43 p.m. on Feb. 1, 1996:

It wasn't entirely my fault.

You probably assume that the act of kicking snow on someone else's windshield is, prima facie, de jure and de facto, wrong, wrong, wrong. Right?

How often we jump to such conclusions when we don't consider all the facts.

First, you may remember, sir, that I was wearing a snappy little Greek seaman's cap pulled down rakishly over my right eye. It was a birthday gift; I had to wear it. When I put it on, I felt Mediterranean and Zorbaesque, not at all myself. Who could hold me responsible for anything I'd do wearing a cap like that?

Second, you may also remember, I had just come out of Kaufman's Furniture at the corner where you were waiting for the traffic light. The problem was not with the store (I often come out of there without kicking snow on windshields) but with my reason for being there.

It was because just the night before, I set my recliner on fire. Well, not on fire actually. There wasn't a flame, just a dull red glow and lots of smoke.

I first smelled it while I was reclining and watching the 6 o'clock news.

"Are you cooking supper tonight, m'love?" I asked my wife. "I smell smoke."

In our division-of-labor arrangement, I put down the toilet seat and cook the supper; she does everything else. If I forget to start supper soon enough, she sometimes puts things in the skillet and burns them to remind me.

“Perhaps a neighbor has a malodorous log on the fire,” she said.

“Well,” I said, “I certainly hope it doesn’t get any stronger.”

I reclined in my recliner again. It got stronger.

“When I recline in my recliner,” I said, “it gets stronger.”

“That’s because,” she observed, “your recliner is smoking.”

“Hah?” I rejoined.

“You are a boob,” she said. “You’ve reclined your recliner right into the hot lightbulb of the reading lamp. There is the beginning of a serious conflagration three inches from your left ear.”

“Like fun,” I said.

“If I weren’t here to notice things for you,” she said, “you’d recline in your recliner smelling smoke until the firemen chopped a hole in the roof. Now we’re going to have to buy a new chair.”

I looked. Sure enough, there was a smoldering hole in the top of the back of the recliner three inches from my left ear. But it wasn’t a large smoldering hole.

“The hole is only as big as a light bulb,” I said, “and if we spray water on it, the chair will be as good as new.”

“No,” she said, “it will never be as good as new. It wasn’t as good as new even when it was new. If you don’t replace the recliner with an expensive and tasteful new one, I believe I shall run off with the milkman.”

“Hah,” I said. “We have no milkman. We’ve had no milkman since 1962.”

“The postman then,” she said. “If you don’t go out and buy a costly new recliner tomorrow, I’ll run off with the postman.”

We have a postman.

So I agreed to Look Around for a new recliner. But not happily.

And I wasn’t happy when I came out of Kaufman’s where I’d been Looking Around. I saw you stopped for your red light at 48th and St. Paul, looking as if you’d never burned a hole in your recliner by reclining it right into a hot lamp.

I don’t mean to be accusatory, sir, but you also had the gall to be driving a wine-colored car, the same color that a friend of mine drives. You had the effrontery to have white hair and a white mustache just like that very friend has. And you must have heard in the barber shop of the legendary witty jokes this friend and I often play on each other—like kicking snow on one another’s windshield.

I thought you were in fact that friend—who only an hour earlier had wittily asked me which piece of furniture I intended to burn today.

That mistaken identity, my distress over having to choose between buying a new recliner and having my wife run off with the postman, my new Greek seaman's cap pulled down rakishly over my right eye—they all came together in irresistible convergance.

I admit that in the split second after I kicked the snow, soccer-style, toward your windshield and before it splatted a few inches in front of your nose, I saw that you had not only white hair and a white mustache, but also a white goatee.

My friend has no goatee. And I had an awful thought: there might be more than one wine-colored car in Lincoln.

That's why you saw me look at my watch and walk briskly back into Kaufman's. I knew they had a back exit.

That's the best case I can make. I suspect that Newt Gingrich is somehow involved—in ways so devious they may not come to light for several more elections. In the meantime, I admit to a certain amount of guilt. I apologize.

But listen: Don't tell my wife about this. Hey?

Millennial Wars

APRIL 21, 1997

Historians in the 21st century don't agree on every aspect of the Great American Millennial Wars. They do agree, though, that the die was cast in the year 2000 when the Hard Rock Lost Lambs o' God used crop dusters to spray Mossback Roman Catholics with a compound that made them allergic to holy water.

They also agree that the seeds of the war had been planted back in 1997.

It was in February of '97 that Judge Roy Moore decided not to obey a higher court ruling that he must remove the Ten Commandments from his Alabama courtroom wall and stop holding prayer meetings with the jury pool.

Judge Moore maintained he was obliged to practice his religion in court.

"My duty under the Constitution is to acknowledge the Judeo-Christian God," he said. But not the deities of religions that don't worship "the God of the Holy Bible on which this country was founded" (*LJS*, April 12, '97).

Alabama Gov. Fob James said that if necessary he'd call out the National Guard to defend Judge Moore's right to be religious in court. The U.S. House of Representatives voted 295-125 to support Judge Moore, and on April 12, 1997, thousands turned out in Montgomery for a rally on his behalf (*LJS*, April 13, '97).

But the real trouble, historians all agree, started a year later in the spring of 1998 when a Southern Baptist judge in Arkansas decided that if a little government establishment of religion was good, a lot would be better. A generalized Judeo-Christian court was too easy: he would set up a specifically Baptist court.

So he installed a baptistry and totally immersed witnesses before they testified. Theological dispute broke out when the courtroom janitor—a suspected Unitarian—grew snappish over cleaning up the splashes on the floor and slipped a quart of indelible blue dye into the baptistry.

Other Arkansas sects, fearful they wouldn't get a fair shake if they refused total immersion, found judges in their congregations who agreed to run courts according to their religious convictions.

The practice spread, and by the beginning of 1999, nearly every denomination in the U.S. had its own home court advantage. A few examples:

• In the Episcopalian court, sessions began with the burning of incense and the ringing of chimes. "Smells and bells," an indignant Quaker snorted.

• In the Mormon court, you couldn't enter unless you arrived in twos and on bicycles.

• In the Presbyterian court, no juries were needed, the verdict having already been predestined.

• In the Lutheran court, sessions began with ritual denunciations of Garrison Keillor, followed by sacramental servings of Jello and Tuna Hot Dish.

• In the Methodist court, witnesses had to repeat the Apostles' Creed, but they didn't have to believe it.

• In the Roman Catholic court, everybody—defendants, plaintiffs, lawyers, onlookers—had to confess. Depending on what they confessed to, they might get anything from life sentences to 20 Hail Marys. In the Mossback Catholic court—Latin only, please—it was 20 Ave Marias.

And it was Latin, all the 21st century historians agree, that precipitated the final breakdown of American unity.

It came when a suit was brought in the Hard Rock Lost Lambs o' God court to do away with the Latin inscription on the Great Seal of the United States, "E pluribus unum." While the notion of "one out of many" was naively noble, albeit secular, it was unacceptable because it was in Latin.

Not just because the Hard Rock Lost Lambs o' God had long since declared English divinely ordained: "If God didn't want His Elect to speak English, why did we grow up talking this way?" It was also because Latin, by long Papist association, was clearly of Satanic origin, and therefore probably unconstitutional. By 2000, almost no one actually read the Constitution any more.

The anti-Latin bias naturally upset the Mossback Catholics and they began showing up on talk shows with Hard Rock Lost Lambs o' God jokes. In Latin, of course. The Elect couldn't understand the jokes, so they assumed the worst.

When their ethnic cleansing attempt—"Send the mackerel-snappers back to Rome!"—failed, their aerial spraying of the Mossbacks began. Massive retaliation ensued: Hard Rock Lost Lambs o' God lay leaders woke up one morning with 666 stenciled on their foreheads.

Soon other sects joined in and the Great American Millennial Wars were on.

By the time the carnage ended in 2020, the United States had disintegrated into 462 separate theocracies.

Judge Roy Moore, alarmed by the furor he'd set off, had converted to Islam and relocated in Iran back in 2002. There he was named the Ayatollah Roy and encouraged to continue his experiments in sectarian jurisprudence, free at last of religious diversity and outmoded ideas about separation of church and state.

Senior Discount

JUNE 2, 1997

"Hah!" I yell to my wife.

I hand her the newspaper and point to the AP story about the geezer who wears dirty jeans and gives away money in Leesburg, Va. His name is Irwin Uran, he's 71, and he's suing a former girlfriend for not returning his cat and his goat.

But that's not why I yell "Hah!"

Nor is it because Irwin Uran lives in a Best Western motel with his dog, Roger, and just gave a million dollars to Leesburg "to help children." Irwin Uran says he has about $400 million.

No, what excites me is a quotation from the proprietor of a bagel shop where Irwin Uran eats bagels: "He always asks for the senior citizen discount."

That's what makes me yell "Hah!" to my wife.

"Let's see," she says without looking up from her crossword puzzle. "That's a 'hah' with an exclamation point rather than a 'hah' with a question mark, so rather than indicating befuddlement it denotes reinforcement of some odd little belief of yours. What is it this time?"

"Oh, not much," I say. "Just another story about a guy who has 400 million smackerooskies because he always asks for the senior citizen discount on his bagel."

My wife is embarrassed when I ask for my senior citizen discount. I'm entitled. She's not. Sometimes I ask for the senior citizen discount for both of us.

"He wears dirty jeans just like mine," I say while she reads the story. "He lives in a Best Western with his dog, Roger. I imagine Best Western has a nice little senior citizen discount, but he could save even more in a little mom-and-pop motel like the one where we stay in Ogallala."

She doesn't like staying in the little mom-and-pop motel in Ogallala, but I work it so I'm driving when we go through there; the rule is that whoever is driving gets to pick the restaurant and the motel.

"Anyway," I say, "it's not staying in the motel that made him rich. It's the bagels. Read the part about the bagels."

She finishes and hands back the the paper.

"Wrong again, Bozo," she says. "Doesn't say Irwin Uran piled up 400 million smackerooskies from senior citizen discounts on his bagels. Says he 'made his fortune investing wisely.' Something you're laughably befuddled about."

"The best offense is defense," I say. "A penny saved is a penny earned."

"Think about it, Mr. Buffett," she says. "Say a bagel sandwich costs $3.60. Say the senior citizen discount is 10 percent. Any idea how many he'd have to eat to save 400 million smackerooskies?"

"Hah?" I say as she whips out her pocket calculator.

"He'd have to eat more than a trillion bagel sandwiches," she says. "If he ate three a day, it would take him more than 370 million days. More than a million years."

"Sure," I say, "make fun of economy. Ridicule thrift. Mock prudence. Had you been born, as I was, in 1934, a poor forlorn Depression Baby, you too would—"

"Have inbibed frugality with my mother's milk?" she says. "Yeah, yeah, yeah. Then I could have been the second tightest wad in town."

"The Depression saved old Irwin Uran," I say. "He was born in the Roaring Twenties and he'd have lived a life of rampant spendthrifthood had it not been for the Depression. Now he's got $400 million and he gets a senior citizen discount."

"Seems strange," she says. "Doesn't it?"

"The cat and the goat?" I say. "Yeah, that's real weird."

"I mean," she says, "it seems strange that someone with $400 million gets a senior citizen's discount."

"He's entitled," I say. Sometimes I have to spell it out for her. "He's 71."

"But you'd think they'd give discounts to people who need them," she says. "People with $400 million don't need them."

"Class warfare!" I yelp. "Galloping bolshevism! Next you'll be saying I don't need a senior citizen discount either."

"When were we the poorest we've ever been?" she asks.

"That's easy, I say. "When we were in our twenties with three babies and a mortgage."

"And when did we have the most money we've ever had?" she asks.

"Right now," I say. "The kids are gone and the mortgage is paid off."

"So doesn't it seem strange that you didn't get a junior citizen discount when you needed it?" she says. "Instead of a senior citizen discount when you don't need it?"

"Hey, this is America," I say. "The more you got, the more you get. It's a wunnerful, wunnerful system."

Patriotism wells up inside me and I burst into song: "The rich get rich and the poor get poorer. In the meantime, in between time, ain't we got fun?"

"Oh Lord," she says, rolling her eyes. "Can we begin the fun by staying in a motel without bugs next time we're in Ogallala?"

It doesn't sound like a question. It sounds like an ultimatum. But I have limits beyond which I won't be pushed.

"Yes, m'love," I say. "If we find a bagel shop with senior citizen discounts."

Seasonal Stupidity

FEBRUARY 24, 1992

I've been in a deep funk for several weeks now, ever since I found out from *Time* that I'm not always hitting on all my mental cylinders. In the intellectual journey of life, I sometimes show up at the wrong gate. My synapses don't always snap.

It was an article about gender differences and it said that males go through hormonal cycles too, not monthly but annually. High testosterone in the fall, low in the spring. That news doesn't bother me. What bothers me is the news that as testosterone rises, intelligence drops. The more male we become, the dumber we get.

"That's news?" my wife says. "Seems to me self-evident, a redundancy, a tautology. It's like saying the more mud you put in your eye the less you see."

"Oh yeah?" I shoot right back at her. "The article also says males are superior to females in spatial logic. We have an impeccable sense of where we are because we had to spatially orient ourselves to the mastodon hunting grounds while you girls tidied up the cave and wondered which way was north."

That's when she brings up that little problem we had in Marshalltown, Iowa, last October. We got lost. I was driving. It was dark and I was taking a shortcut another guy told me about. Her position was that we should stay on the road we already knew; my position was where would we be if Columbus had done that instead of discovering India? When the shortcut got really dark and narrow, her position was that we should turn around and go back to the road we already knew; my position was that all we had to do was follow the semi in front of us because truck drivers always know where they're going.

This one was going home. He pulled up in front of a house on a deadend street, took out his suitcase, and went inside. So we turned around and tried to find our way back to the road we already knew. It took a while and my wife made comments.

Now she calls that the Great Navigational Black Hole of Marshalltown.

"Don't get too close to Marshalltown," she tells our sons, "or your male spatial logic will get sucked into the Great Navigational Black Hole there."

Then she laughs. She's easily amused.

But I feel better now that I've read the *Time* piece. Remember, Marshalltown was in October. The high testosterone-low intelligence season. Not my fault. Part of Nature's plan. Less than a month later I read an AP story that said males should wait until spring to take their SATs and I was feeling so wolfy I didn't get it. I had a strong urge to hunt mastodon, so I did what seemed like the next best thing: I broke up some concrete with my 16-pound sledge hammer and got a bad backache. It felt good. November. Football season. Yee haw.

But I'm seeing things more clearly now; it's late February and the testosterone is falling and I'm getting smarter. And here's what puts me in a funk: election year politics. The spring primaries are as good as it's going to get. Within the next two or three months the male politicians will be as smart as they're going to be. And by the general election in November, they'll be at their dumbest.

That explains Michael Dukakis sounding like a plausible candidate in the 1988 spring primaries, then in the fall having his picture taken pretending to drive a tank, his head rattling around inside an oversized helmet, grinning like the town loony.

That explains George Bush being able to detect "voodoo" when he was running against Reaganomics in the spring primaries of 1980, then in the fall of 1988 chanting like a witch doctor: "Read my lips; no new taxes. Read my lips; no new taxes."

But my wife tells me not to worry my pretty little head over the fall election. It'll be painless, she says.

"By then," she tells me, patting me on the hand, "it'll be that time of year and you won't understand what's going on anyway."

She says that half the population will be so testosterone-logged by November that we'll be thinking—she's not sure that's the right word—that, hey, the Pledge of Allegiance really is a great campaign issue, and golly, wouldn't it be neato-jet to invade somebody and bust up their sidewalks with 16-pound sledge hammers?

She also says there's an alternative: run Barbara Bush against Hillary Clinton and disinfranchise anyone who sets off the alarm in the testosto-detector tunnels we'll make everyone walk through to get to the voting booths. But where in this land, she asks with that flawed spatial logic of hers, is there a party hack free enough of his glands to see the wisdom of that?

Waiting for Carlos

OCTOBER 19, 1998

I've been waiting for him for a decade or two when he finally shows up in my Freshman English class. He's a little wiry guy in a red and black plaid shirt, faded jeans, and a baseball cap, bill to the front. He's flopped in his chair, but he looks interested, and his name jumps off the class roster: Carlos Camacho.

I assign the Handy-Dandy Six-Part Ciceronian Argument. The six parts have nifty Latin names: *exordium, narratio, divisio, confirmatio, refutatio, peroratio.*

The class groans. Carlos still looks interested.

Done well, the assignment can result in a tightly organized piece of formulaic writing, almost always in a turgid style with nothing of the writer's own voice showing through. Rhetorical castor oil, I tell myself. Good for freshmen.

Carlos uses the assignment to attack the assignment. Formulaic writing, he writes, is never worth reading. Why, he writes, wouldn't an experienced teacher know that?

But his insubordination is a ruse. His argument against the assignment follows precisely the assigned form, the six parts all in prescribed order, all doing exactly what they're supposed to do. And the Latin is spelled right.

"Who is this guy?" I say aloud as I enter his A in the gradebook.

Later in the semester, I tell them to write research papers, complete with MLA documentation and evidence that they know their way around the library. They choose the subject. Carlos wants to do his on how Tom Osborne recruits.

"Hey," I say, "this counts a third of your grade. This is serious stuff."

"Tom Osborne's recruiting," he says, "is a serious subject."

So he writes a paper on how Tom Osborne recruits, impeccably documented and researched, including a telephone interview with The Man Himself. Even I am interested in it. Another A.

"Carlos Camacho," I say to everyone, "should be an English major."

A year later, he's in my Advanced Composition class where we all read aloud what we've written. The assignment is to write in someone else's narrative voice. Carlos has just read "Catcher in the Rye," so he becomes Holden Caulfield.

"If you really want to know about it, you'll probably want to hear about how I came to Wesleyan and all, but I really don't feel like getting into that crap," he writes in flawless Holdenese. He goes on to talk about the class itself.

The instructor, he writes, "is about 400 years old and all he does is drone on in class about these corny writing assignments so much I want to puke. Boy, but the other phonies all eat it up. Like you're supposed to commit suicide or something if you can't get the damn assignment down right. Sometimes I'll sort of horse around with old Satterfield and do it wrong on purpose, just for fun."

Then he devotes a paragraph to each of the others in the class, ending with one on Carlos himself, whose papers, he writes, are always too long:

"I'm not kidding. He'll sit there and read for about ten hours. I've dropped him about a thousand hints after class that maybe he was boring all of us, and that it never exactly broke our hearts when he was done, but he never gets it."

We all laugh and laugh.

Carlos becomes an English major. He goes to Stratford and London with Anne and Roger Cognard to sniff out Shakespeare's spoor. He comes back this fall for his last year at Wesleyan. He's going to write a piece of fiction for his senior project. He asks me to be one of his readers.

Here's where the narrative goes to past tense. Here's where it gets grim.

Carlos' funeral was last week, 60 or 70 years too soon. He died in a house fire across the street from the campus. Funeral flowers piled up in the Old Main office and nothing in the building was the same.

Me, for instance.

Carlos corrupted me. He goosed me into three of the seven deadly sins:

- Pride, at the wonderful things he wrote in my class, things I could pretend to be partly responsible for, although "teaching" Carlos to write was simply giving him an assignment and getting the hell out of his way.

• Envy, because I saw in him what I would like to have been at his age.

• Anger, because teachers live in part through the lives of their students, and now that Carlos' life is gone, I've been cosmically cheated.

There's been some terrible misunderstanding of the regulation that students are forbidden to die before their teachers—a sub-section of the regulation that children are forbidden to die before their parents.

I will not accept it.

Through my office window, I see a student half a block away, a little wiry guy in jeans and plaid shirt and baseball cap, bill to the front. He's coming this way. I wait for a knock at my door. High time we talked about the senior project.

I wait, but there is no knock. The burned-out house across the street mocks me, and I'm waiting, waiting.

Daniel and Agnes Freeman Homesteaders. On January 1, 1863, Daniel Freeman filed the first homestead in the United States. This book by his great-granddaughter Beverly S. Kaplan tells the story of not only his property near Beatrice, Nebraska, but of the nearly desert land, the pioneers and their struggle to make the "free land" a home, the first house, the railroads and the politics of the era. 8"×5" 187 pages 26-X $9.95

In All Its Fury. The story of the Great Blizzard of 1888. This storm, which covered nearly a third of the nation, roared down from Canada at 50 miles an hour, dropped temperatures 36 degrees, and killed more than 1,000 people, is described through the eyes of survivors. These accounts of heroism and courage were collected by W. H. O'Gara of Laurel, Nebraska, in 1947.
9"×6" 343 pages 04-9 $9.95

The Lay of the Land: A View From the Prairie. Brent Olson. With hunger, love and poignancy, a philosopher farmer's elegant essays distill the essence of life in the Great Plains. Olson farms the land settled by his Norwegian immigrant great-grandparents and lives in the house they built. Savor his views on life one by one, or wolf them down at one sitting. This is soul-nourishing stuff. For fans of Garrison Keillor, Henry David Thoreau and Tom Bodett. 5¼"×7⅛" 36-7 $11.95

Lincoln: The Prairie Capital. This 124-page book by Jim McKee tells the history of Nebraska's capital city with interesting accounts, stories and hundreds of photos. McKee recounts Lincoln's past from the tiny village of 30 with "no water power, mines, fuel, nor other so-called natural advantages" to the modern city of nearly 180,000, punctuating historical facts and formalities with how-it-happened anecdotes.
8½"×11" 124 pages 07-3 $17.95

Luther North, Frontier Scout. Jeff O'Donnell. The scouts, who made the frontier railroads and settlement possible, were "one of the most thrilling chapters of Nebraska history." The story of Luther North, as told here, was one of the most fascinating links in the winning of the west. 5½"×8½" 216 pages 10-3 $13.95

Miss Adams, Country Teacher. At age 18 on March 1, 1928, Treva Adams Strait began teaching in a one-room converted cowboy's shack 35 miles from town on the western Nebraska prairie. Award-winning author Strait tells the story of her early teaching career and pre-depression life in Nebraska in a fascinating narrative suitable for all ages. 6"×9" 25-1 $8.95

Nebraska Place Names was researched for 17 years by Elton Perkey. This completely indexed book first appeared serially in "Nebraska History" and has been completely corrected and brought up to date. Entries for each town and county include populations, dates of establishment and discontinuance as well as notes on the origin of site names.
8½"×11" 226 pages 19-7 $12.95

Oh Grandma, You're Kidding. Gladys Douglass recounts eighty years of memories of growing up in Nebraska, told in humorous and interesting detail. Covering everyday life in the Great Plains and how it was survived, 30 chapters include: Before TV and Radio; Woman's Work; Baked Beans on Washday; Riding the Train; Dollar Day At The Fair; Omaha's Easter Tornado; and Seeing Halley's Comet. A fascinating recounting for those who "remember when" or those unable to recall life before TV. 110 pages 00-6 $7.95

Omaha Tribal Myths and Trickster Tales. Roger Welsch. Over 70 Omaha Indian tales featuring "Trickster" in his many guises are retold with annotations at the end of each story. These fables will help the reader appreciate the rich culture of the Omaha well before "civilization" was forced on them by white soldiers and missionaries. 6"×9" 285 pages 11-1 $14.95

Pinnacle Jake + Pinnacle Jake's Roundup. As told to Nellie Snyder Yost. 84 years worth of vivid recollections from A. B. "Pinnacle Jake" Snyder on what cowboy life was really like at the turn of the century. J. Frank Dobie said it is "one of the best range books I have read . . ." Includes nearly 100 pages of new—never before published—pages of Great Plains range life tales.
8"×5" 340 pages 28-6 $12.95

SHIP TO:

Name____

Address ______________________________________

City ________________________ State_______ Zip ____________

All orders shipped postpaid. Nebraska residents add appropriate sales tax.

ISBN prefix is 0-934904

MAIL ORDERS TO:

J.L. Lee Co.

LEE BOOKSELLERS
281 East Park Plaza • 66th & "O" Streets • 56th & Hwy. 2
LINCOLN, NEBRASKA 68505
(402) 467-4416 • toll free 1-888-665-0999
e-mail leebooks@binary.net